Dogmatic *vs* Biblical Theology

Dogmatic
vs
Biblical
Theology

edited by

HERBERT VORGRIMLER

HELICON

Baltimore - Dublin

Helicon Press, Inc.
1120 N. Calvert Street
Baltimore, Maryland 21202

Library of Congress Catalog Card Number 64-24242

First published in German by
Matthias-Grünewald-Verlag, Mainz, 1962

Nihil Obstat: CARROLL E. SATTERFIELD
         Censor Librorum

Imprimatur: ✠LAWRENCE J. SHEHAN, D.D.
         Archbishop of Baltimore
         July 31, 1964

The *Nihil Obstat* and *Imprimatur* are official declarations that a book
or pamphlet is free of doctrinal or moral error. No implication is
contained therein that those who have granted the *Nihil Obstat* and
Imprimatur agree with the opinions expressed.

PRINTED IN THE REPUBLIC OF IRELAND BY
HELY THOM LIMITED, DUBLIN

FOREWORD

Ever since the great days of scholastic theology, dogmatic theology and exegesis have tended to go their own ways. In this century they have even clashed, to the special hurt of young theologians and all those who listen to sermons.

Now, however, the suspicions which marked this clash are dissolving, and the necessary bridge is being built from both sides. And though this bridge is not yet complete, this collection of essays will indicate just how far the work has progressed. It is clear that even dogmatic theology is still in course of evolution, and that its exponents do not enjoy the infallibility which belongs to the Church as such and to her teaching office. It is also clear that exegesis, in the greatly changed form in which it appears in this century, is likewise still seeking for self-understanding. This volume exhibits the two great fields of work. We see basic principles being weighed: on the one hand, the scientific character of dogmatics and exegesis, the essential nature of biblical theology, and on the other the immense field of particular questions—here presented in some striking examples—in which exegesis and dogmatics have to listen to each other. The original German publishers, Matthias-Grünewald, must be credited with thinking of a selective publication in which much that was buried in technical periodicals could be made available to a larger circle of readers. In addition, we are very glad that we can offer some essays here published for the first time, together with the revision of some older ones. The special nature of this collection of essays is symbolic of what is happening between exegesis and dogmatics. Many things stand side by side without connexion with each other. But the conversation has begun, and what we aim at with this collection of essays touches at one point decisively with the object of the Second Vatican Council. The Church must, as John XXIII strove to realize in word and deed, be renewed in the spirit of open-hearted honesty, of love and brotherliness, for the sake of its own members and for the sake of the testimony demanded of it for the world. The great hope of the younger theologians is that in the future too, the discussion of the problems here laid bare will be carried on in this spirit and in freedom.

HERBERT VORGRIMLER

Freiburg i. Br., 18 July 1962

CONTENTS

Dogmatic *vs* Biblical Theology

Karl
Hermann
Schelkle

SACRED SCRIPTURE
AND WORD OF GOD

We call Sacred Scripture God's word. But when we try
to catch this word in the Scripture what do we hear? Not
the direct *word* in the helpful evidence of divine and life-
laden truth; directly, only the *Scripture* is given us, one
book among many, and indeed a book, as regards the New
Testament at any rate, that has no claim at all to be placed
among the great works of literature. Among the books left
to us by Greek antiquity, the New Testament is rather
insignificant from the literary point of view. How poor is
the Scripture beside the riches and brilliance of Plato! A
man like St Augustine, who was a master of the culture
and art of language, as well as a passionate reader of the
Bible, could pronounce his expert verdict on Sacred Scripture in these words: 'Ignoble it appeared to me beside the
nobility of Cicero' (*Confessions* 3, 5).

As far as form is concerned, Sacred Scripture addresses
the reader directly only in small sections; for the most part
it is much more a narrative of something that happened in
the far distant past. And its component parts are not

harmonized with each other according to any well thought out plan. This Scripture is a collection, often accidental, of books which each have their own special origin. Each book was written to serve a peculiar historical situation. Understandably therefore, the writings are affected by ideas and attitudes of the past, and are even subject to intellectual and moral imperfection in the very form of their words and text.

Only gradually were the books gathered together. In many instances, the Church was in doubt for centuries whether some among them were to be reckoned as part of Scripture at all. Historians of religion—rightly, from their stand-point—have ranged the sacred book of the Christian faith along with the sacred books of other religions, and our Sacred Scripture can appear strangely interchangeable with other religious texts. The historical research and criticism of the last century has made all this unquestionable and harshly clear to us. Our task is not to deny or conceal this fact, but to stand firm against it. Sacred Scripture shares the hazards and limitations of everything human. 'Even St John has told us not how this can be, but only how he could speak of it, being a man talking about God' (St Augustine, *on John* 1:1). Indeed, the word of God seems often to be proposed in such a way that it can hardly defend itself any more against questions, doubts, contradiction, and even ridicule.

Yet the community of those who hold the Christian faith—understood here as extending far beyond any *one* Church as delimited by its profession of faith—maintains as its conviction and experience that Scripture is God's word, the word which came and still comes forth from God and gives testimony about God, which is revelation.

What does this Christian conviction mean? The Gospel

of St John (1 : 1) begins: 'In the beginning was the Word, and the Word was with God, and the Word was God.' From all eternity God has within him the Word which utters and expresses him. But the Word was also in the world, as its light and life. At last it 'became flesh and dwelt amongst us'. To this Word of God the Scriptures testify, and the Gospel speaks of the Word of God made man, and the epistles of the Apostles expound it. Because the Word of God was always in the world, and because it became man, men can have word of God and speak of God to one another. And this word comes in all simplicity and clarity, really a *word*, not just guess-work or stammering, which is all that would be rightly due to man in face of God.

Christ is God's word to the world. He can say: 'Truly, we speak what we know, and give testimony to what we have seen' (Jn 3 : 11). Christ, as this definitive word of God, sustains also what God said earlier to the world, and guarantees all that went before, since he perfects it, according to the word of the Apostle: 'In the Son of God came the great Yes. All the promises of God that there were, in him is the Yes' (2 Cor 1 : 19f).

The Scripture is word about God's being and life. It is also word about the world, since the world is conceived of as God's creation precisely in the Scripture. And this creation is not thought of merely in its first moment, but as God's work which he sustains at every moment and into whose history he ever reaches. Thereby Scripture is also God's word about every man in his own time.

Because Scripture contains the teaching of Christ, it is the true word of God and about God. But it contains not merely the word of Christ, but Christ, himself, the Word. Scripture is his body, says the theology of the

Fathers. So Origen says: 'The Scriptures are one single perfect body of the Word' (*Homilies on Jeremias*, Fragment 2, *Griechische Christliche Schriftsteller* 13, p. 197). Scripture is an incarnation of the eternal Christ, comparable to his embodiment in the Eucharist and in the Church. All such embodiment of the Lord however is that, ever-present, of the Christ, who is now the Spirit (2 Cor 3 : 17). The Scripture is therefore filled by the living God. The faith expresses this as the doctrine of the inspiration of Sacred Scripture. And it is precisely with reference to inspiration that the teaching Church proclaims Scripture as the word of God: 'Written under the inspiration of the Holy Spirit, the Scriptures have God as their author' (Vatican I, Session 3, ch. 2).

Inspiration does not mean only the inerrancy of the Scriptures. A book can be free of error and yet not be inspired. Inspiration is also not merely an event of the past which has been terminated. It means something permanent in Scripture, its supremely present spiritual force, its power, that is, as God's word 'to be living and effective and sharper than any two-edged sword, piercing to the division of soul and spirit into thought and marrow, and judge over the movements and thoughts of the heart' (Heb 4 : 12).

Scripture is therefore not merely the self-expression of the moral or religious man in the successive stages of his evolution. It is the form the Word of God takes in writing and truly the original document of God. However, when we approach it, we do not find it as the word of God addressed to us, but as the story of the past words and actions of God among other men. So the question becomes this: How can I perceive the Scripture not just as testimony and word about me, but as addressed to me?

We already find it difficult to interpret the word of any book separated from us by thousands of years in such a way that its living force is set free to captivate us. The task of making the word of God audible to us from the pages of Scripture must be all the harder, since as we have seen, though it is the word of God, it does not appear in majesty but in the form of a slave. It comes concealed and disguised, like that great utterance of God to the world which is Christ. An ancient hymn which St Paul found already in use in the Church, and which he adopted into the epistle to the Philippians, runs as follows: 'Being in the form of God, he did not hold fast to equality with God, but emptied himself, taking the form of a slave, when he appeared as man. He humbled himself even to the death of the cross' (Phil 2:6–11). So, the theologians say, the word in the book, *logos embiblos,* is also hidden and without its true form, just like the Word in the flesh, *logos ensarkos,* who is the central truth of the Scripture. Indeed precisely because Scripture is testimony to the Word of God in the flesh, its divine vitality and truth must be beyond proof, to be reached and experienced only by the faith which dares to surrender itself to it.

Ultimately therefore, the word is only accessible and audible in the decision of faith, a decision which must constantly be made and is never finally accomplished but must always be begun again anew. Of course, this act of hearing is not something that can be done once and for all. It must be done again and again, little by little, after the manner of Isaias 50:4, 'Morning after morning he awakens my ear, that I may hearken like a disciple'.

But to go the road to the decision of faith, the road from the reading of Scripture to the hearing of the word, and to reach our goal, which is to hear, two aids are offered us. Of this help we shall speak in what follows. They are assistance of very different kinds, but they must be mentioned together. One is the aid of scientific exegetical effort, the other is the aid of the community of believers.

Before we try to read the Scripture and to hear the word, we must consider something quite fundamental. As members of the Christian Church, we suffer from the disadvantage that constant repetition of the same passages of the Bible means that they are all too easily read and heard in haste, and not in depth. The sayings and stories have been known too long. Our ears are stopped, and we can no longer perceive the novelty and the strangeness, the beauty and the seriousness of the message. This makes it very hard for us to hear the living word from the pages of Scripture. What we need, constantly and above all, is true human sensibility, which is open to the variety, the fulness, the real incredibility of Scripture. It would be already an advantage if we could manage, when we open the book, to forget for once how we have heard the passage in long years of habit. Otherwise we succumb to the temptation of taking in only certain passages of Scripture which suit us, always in the same key. In fact, the word of Scripture in its totality is very different from many of the ordinary views and habits of Christian faith and life. We read the Scripture fruitfully only in so far as this divergence becomes clear to us. Only then can it renew and mould our faith and our life. Before this moment we are masters of Scripture, because we dispose of it. Only then does it become our master and we become subject to its word. Only when we have first made a stranger of the text can it become truly close to us.

The first help in understanding the text is given us by the scientific efforts of exegesis. Luther was right when he spoke of the sheath of language in which the sword of the word of God is kept. The New Testament is an ancient Greek text. The Bible poses therefore many questions, as every ancient Greek text does: textual criticism and restoration of the original; grammar, vocabulary and meaning to be explored in depth; the psychology of prophets, Apostles and preachers of the word to be examined at least to the point where they can claim that 'the spiritual man is judged by nobody'!

We have learnt that an intimate knowledge of the Judaeo-Aramaic and Greek languages, and of the culture, spirituality and religion during the centuries at the watershed of time is absolutely necessary for the understanding of the New Testament. We have first the legislation and the prophecies of the Old Testament, then the New Testament. But between them come rabbinical Judaism and the rich post-canonical literature, with its piety based on the Law, a deep sense of sin, and an imminent expectation of redemption. Very often these writings tell us more about the real and immediate background of the New Testament than do the canonical books of the Old Testament. Undreamt-of information has been given us by the recent discovery of the writings of the Qumran community by the Dead Sea. Likewise, much false interpretation of the Greek New Testament is due to its being compared too closely to classical antiquity. The New Testament lives in the daily life of the Hellenistic world, in its houses, markets, courts and temples. This is not the world of 'classical Greece'. It is Greek life as it was when it became the current, world-wide culture of the Hellenistic age. The effort to become acquainted with all this clearly belongs to the study of history and the ancient classical languages. But such an effort is indispensable and exegesis can take

2

none of it for granted. It is for scientific theology to do this work on behalf of the whole Church, which wishes to read and hear Scripture.

While doing this work, exegetes must not only note the proximity, the relations, the connexions of the New Testament with outside spirituality and religion. They must also, and much more, mark the opposition which denotes the uniqueness and the novelty of the word of revelation. Thus exegetes must take soundings, with the help of all the instruments of linguistic science, in a multitude of words and concepts if they are to allow themselves the hope of hearing the one important word. They will recognize that this unique word is indeed a sound in the streets of this world: but that it has, in its novelty and totality, something that cannot be understood as part of this world.

Such study of the Bible has been using its own methods, often mechanical and statistical but thereby all the more reliable, to impart to us information which is not only interesting but theologically valuable. To choose but one example, we know that the whole of Greek writing, outside the Bible, does not know the word *agape*, 'love'. The Septuagint, the Greek translation of the Old Testament, imported the word into biblical Greek, apparently from the popular Greek spoken in Egypt. This means that the translators chose a word not hitherto used in the literary language, because its meaning had not been fixed by a pre-history of philosophical and literary usage. They were thus free to give it a new content. (The full proof of this is given by C. Spicq in *Agape*, 1955.) The word *agape* was new to Greek antiquity, just as the thing itself was new to it. Thus the statistics of language does its part to explain the word of our Lord: 'A *new* commandment I give unto you, that you love one another' (Jn 13 : 34).

Most words used in the Bible, of course, are also in common usage in profane Greek, as statistics show. But the meaning in which they occur often varies decisively. What St Paul meant by 'grace', 'faith', 'justice', 'revelation', 'Spirit', and 'Church' had hitherto never been heard in such words by the Greeks, nor even the Jews. And New Testament Greek is not the lofty speech of classical Greece, but the everyday language of the Hellenistic age. Adolf Deissmann, to whom we owe much of our understanding of New Testament Greek, speaks of the insight this understanding gives us: 'Thus it becomes clear that the Gospel belongs to the poor and simple. To these was it brought and in their language was it written, just as it was listened to by them, and just as it can and must be proclaimed to them once more. We feel that for shepherds here is the chief shepherd, for sailors here is the pilot, for wanderers here is the leader, for warriors here is the general. For farmers, Jesus will bless the seed. Invited every day to our table, he will sit with us as our guest and break bread with us' (*Licht vom Osten* 4, 1923).

But linguistic research and literary criticism can and must bring us further. A book which really has something to say is not just the total of its words. Beyond that, it is one particular word, which seeks to evoke a response in the reader. In fact, the real and permanent task of history is not to acquaint us with past things and spoken words, but with ourselves. This it does by demanding from us a decision with regard to all the words and events narrated. The exponents of the ancient classics, for instance, have always felt that they must explain Greek tragedy in such a way that we may hear and understand in it the tragedy of all human existence. Plato is fully propounded only when we are forced to make a decision about the eternal claims of the ideal, which no one ever urged more nobly than he. And what is this one word of Scripture? In the Old Testament it is clearly that God is the Creator and Father, the Judge, the Lord, the Saviour. But the word from the New Testament is the persuasion of unbelief, and the conviction that brings faith in Father, Son and Spirit. This is the final word. A purely historical investigation can—and indeed must—make it audible, if it is to do its full duty by the Greek book. This, to be sure, is the dividing-line. Historical interpretation can make the contents and the claims of the word of Scripture audible. But to say yes or no to it is each one's personal decision.

Tribulation can be brought on individual and Church alike by this work of exegesis on Scripture. The New Testament already knew this. The second epistle of St Peter, written in late apostolic times, tells how the Church is disturbed and oppressed by contradictory interpretations of Scripture. 'Our beloved brother Paul, in accordance with the wisdom given him, has written in the same way in all his letters where he speaks of these things. Some of which is hard to understand, and ignorant, unstable readers wrest it, as they do the rest of the Scriptures, to their own destruction' (2 Pt 3: 15f). Since the word is in written form, its exegesis is unavoidably necessary, and this again has its unavoidable and often difficult set of problems.

The work of linguistic and historical research on the Scriptures may often have erred dangerously. Often there have been complaints that such work disturbs the Church. But we owe not a little to its painstaking efforts. To it we owe our knowledge of the history of the salvific word and work of God in the Old Testament. To it we owe our true historical knowledge of the primitive Church. To it we owe the historical understanding of the sacred origins of that faith and life, full of creative force, of which we are the heirs.

Consider one of the most recent and important discoveries of such research. The Gospel and primitive Christianity were filled with the urgent expectation of the kingdom of God. Hence we know that all Christianity, if indeed it wishes to be biblical, must be filled with the same expectation of the 'last things'. Further, careful analytical research has taught us that, on the whole, our ordinary picture of the homogeneity of Scripture is due to our co-ordinating all the sayings that can be made fit into one another. But the apparent homogeneity is very deceptive. Scripture is in fact full of the most difficult contrasts, each one pregnant with evolution, and the unity of Scripture is to be sought at a deeper level. Its unity is not the easy harmony of events and words, but only the deep unity of God himself, which is not comprehensible to man.

To man, God is the God of mysteries and contrasts; and such too is Scripture. It mocks at all the art of harmonizing. This, along with its 'form of the slave', is what conceals the glory of its truth beneath the darkness of contradictions. And these contradictions are not to be solved by any system of mere human logic, ethics and religion. Let us remember the biblical 'for us', which means that every man is in fact decisively affected by what once happened on the Cross. Let us remember the contrasts worked out so forcibly by St Paul: predestination and liberty, works and grace, the impotence of man and his responsibility before God.

The Christian faith is not, however, a doctrine made up of pure ideas, it is the message about the event of salvation. It is not merely the preaching of the word, it is the announcement of certain facts. Indeed, this is the very word which is to be proclaimed: that the word of grace has gone forth and that salvation has come to pass in the reality of history. St Paul makes it clear (1 Cor 15: 12–19) that the faith stands or falls by the reality of the historical resurrection. Yet anything that claims to be history must be open to historical research. Hence the grave problems that can arise at this point are authentic questions, not idle inventions. To attend to them is not a sign of unbelief but the obligation of sincerity. To forbid the freedom of this questioning would rather point to unbelief. For it is only unbelief which cannot trust the word of God to stand fast in face of serious questioning. Strictly scientific work on the Bible, as it has been done and is being done, has on the contrary received its blessing and will go on receiving it, the blessing of a deeper understanding of man's share in the Scriptures, and also the blessing of a true understanding of the word of God, which was uttered through the words of men.

The other aid to hearing and understanding Scripture is the community of the faithful, the community of the Church. Living tradition is of decisive importance for the understanding of every piece of writing that has come down to us. We take up Plato or Virgil in a different way from Buddha or the Koran. Clearly, from the first, it is the tradition of western humanism which transmits to us, in immeasurable depths, our first and last understanding of Greek philosophy or Latin poetry. And what would Sacred Scripture be without the history of its effects, without the fellowship of the Church to testify to its unity? Would it not be a miscellany of seemingly haphazard books, of words and stories full of beneficent, but also of destructive force? 'The fact remains,' says von Drey, 'that Scripture has been given many interpretations and must therefore be open to many interpretations.' Church history shows how often and how banefully Scripture has been misread and misapplied in the hands of fanatics.

The living tradition of the Church is not confined to an oral tradition which completes Scripture on a few small points. Neither is it the Church in the organization of her teaching office, explaining this or that word of the Bible by a dogmatic definition. Tradition is the whole living Church as manifestation of the Spirit and the Power (1 Cor 2:4), the living testimony of the faith of the community, through which new faith is ever being born. And Church in this sense is not merely *one* communion. We do not mean only the Roman Church, but the *Una Sancta Catholica*. We acknowledge gladly and thankfully how much we have gained from our Evangelical brethren, precisely in explaining Scripture. And we testify that it is our hope that the Churches which have been separated for 400 years on account of the Book, may be ever more and more ready to hear the one word of God about the Book.

This common testimony is given in the preaching of the Church, as it explains the words and the message in ever new terms. It comes likewise as the word is testified to in prayer and the celebration of the liturgy. Following St Augustine, and carrying his formula further, one speaks gladly of the Sacrament as the *verbum visibile*, and of the word as the *sacramentum audible* (*Patrologia Latina*, 35, 1840; 42, 365 f; 37, 969). According to the Apostle, the liturgy is the proclamation of the death of the Lord, in the presence of his Cross, till he comes (1 Cor 11:26). How inexhaustibly deep and salutary is the representation of the Passion and Resurrection of the Lord in the liturgy of Holy Week and of Easter Week! There is one single essential element, above all else, which the liturgy presents in unique and convincing truth: the presence of the living Lord who is the Spirit. Thereby the Church has always held fast to the whole Gospel, even in times when exegesis of the Book broke down.

'The essential content of Sacred Scripture is always present to the Church, because it is her life-blood, her soul, her breath, her all' (Möhler, *Symbolik*, par. 42). We comprise all that as tradition under the statement of the Council of Trent, and later of the Vatican: 'that in matters of faith and morals we must hold as the true sense of Sacred Scripture that which Mother Church has held and holds. Therefore no one is allowed to interpret Sacred Scripture contrary to this sense or contrary to the unanimous and universal consent of the Fathers'.

The interpretation offered by the Fathers is therefore the classical doctrine of the Church and of theology. But entrance to their world is difficult, and long efforts are needed to gain it. Here too, and precisely here, scientific theology has much to do. The Councils speak of the 'unanimous teaching' of the Fathers. But such unanimity is only seldom demonstrable and rarely accessible. Often, after research into the ancient exegesis of a text of Scripture, it appears that what was accepted as the common teaching of the Fathers was only ostensibly so. Far from being unanimous doctrine, it was the exegesis of a single Father or school which, for some reason or other or even by accident, had become the prevalent exegesis. Further, the Fathers did not use our methods of historical criticism. And the tireless efforts of scientific historians have won for us results which even in the field of biblical exegesis are of immense value, and now indispensable.

True, we have learnt the dangers and illusions of historicism as well as the value of historical research. Biblical exegesis knows well how slavery to the letter of history can hinder and even destroy a true understanding of history. We also begin to suspect, once again, how antiquity and the Middle Ages, sensitive to the symbolical meaning of all nature and history, could find an approach to the truth which is closed to us. Such an exegesis of Scripture sees nature and history imbued and borne onwards by the *one* God who is Creator and Redeemer. Since he is one, he is always and everywhere manifest in words and actions, dimensions and signs, which have a constant resemblance to one another. Thus one can be symbol of another: word for word, thing for thing, man for man, history for history and finally Testament for Testament. Hence St Augustine calls 'the whole creation's beauty the great poem of the inexpressible Creator' (*Ep* 138, 5). And St Bonaventure, the great medieval symbolist commentator, says: 'That which has been created can be comprehended either as a thing or a sign' (see E. Gilson, *Bonaventure*, 1929).

Let us take one example of such interpretation. In Psalm 90 the Fathers read, as we do, 'With his pinions he covers thee and under his wings thou findest refuge'. From the earliest times (Hippolytus, *de Antichristo*, 61; St Ambrose, *on Psalm* 118; St Augustine, *on Psalm* 90), the Fathers understood these pinions as an image of the arms of Christ spread out on the Cross, and as a proclamation of the Cross. Not as if the psalmist had already thought of the cross of Christ. But only through the Cross was the truth of the Psalm revealed. The words are an absolute guarantee of God's protection of his servants. But are they really

fulfilled? In this world and age, all appearances often tell
against it. But the promise is true when understood in the
light of the Cross. Here it promises God's fidelity, abiding,
rescuing even when bodily life perishes. Our methods of
history and philology may no longer be adapted to such
an exegesis. But it is still unquestionably valid, for here
spirit meets spirit, the Spirit of Scripture meets the same
Spirit of the faithful, and they recognize each other with
certainty.

Tradition explains Scripture to us. Tradition existed
before Scripture and transmits to us Scripture to-day. The
Church knew and knows, even without Scripture, what
it believes. Yet Scripture, in face of Tradition, retains its
primary value and dignity. As God's word, it is independent in its own right and does not receive its authority from
the Church. The Church is the agent and dispenser of the
word, just as she is the agent and dispenser of the sacraments. The Church and her tradition are themselves bound
to the word of Scripture. Tradition is not independent
but, as it is formed and developed, Scripture constantly
penetrates it and forms it also.

Humanly speaking, tradition left to itself might be in
danger of corrupting the word of God by the word of
man, just as Jesus reproaches the Pharisees for their
hypocritical abandonment of the commandment of God,
to put their own tradition and the tradition of men in its
place (Mk 7:6-9). The Church needs the true, pure word
of God, which is addressed to her through the Scriptures,
in order to be constantly purified, judged, nourished, con-
soled and saved. The New Testament is the oldest document of the Church. Here the faith, life, essence and spirit
of the Church are attested and described in the pure
original perfection of the beginning. Now in every spirit-

ual movement, the origins are normative for all the future, and its life remains authentic and vigorous only in so far as it always draws new strength from its beginnings and from its roots. So too Scripture, as 'Word of life' (Jn 5: 24), life-giving like the Sacrament, is constantly creating the Church.

It remains however that the explanation of Scripture in the Church is determined and bound by tradition. But then it should be bound for the sake of the brethren. St Paul says (1 Cor 8: 13) that though he would never give up his freedom in the matter, he would abstain from meat for ever, if the brother for whom Christ died were to suffer harm otherwise. Scripture means life for the Church, and exegesis is therefore not only a scientific question, but always a vital question for the Church, and a matter of conscience therefore for interpreter and hearer. Interpretation and hearing are not to destroy the Scripture and the Church; rather, they must build up the community. For it is more important 'to utter words of edification, exhortation and consolation for men' than to speak in tongues of science and ecstasy (1 Cor 14: 3f).

We know well, and many of our exegetes think of it with painful anxiety, that this link between interpretation and tradition could narrow and hamper, whatever the inadequacies and misunderstandings at work, the field of enquiry and research, of explanation and understanding. But the bond is there also for the sake of the inviolable validity of the word. For it is a bond which also sets free. As the community of all Christian times and peoples, the Church can free men from hazard, from the tyranny of a single, perhaps outstanding interpreter, as well as from the overwhelming force of any temporary stage and movement of cultural history.

Scriptural interpretation in the Church gives instead a share in the knowledge of the whole fellowship of the saints. What single mind would be deep and broad enough to come near to the immensity and fulness of Scripture? We may here quote the last words which Martin Luther wrote, on a slip of paper, before his death: 'No one can understand the Bucolics of Virgil unless he has been five years a shepherd. No one can understand the Georgics of Virgil unless he has been five years a farmer. No one can fully understand the letters of Cicero unless he has moved about in a great society for five and twenty years. Let no one think he has sufficiently tasted the Scriptures unless he has ruled the churches for a hundred years with prophets like Elias and Eliseus, with John the Baptist, with Christ and the Apostles. We are beggars. That is true'.

The emphasis on the fact that Scripture and its interpretation must serve the Church does not introduce a foreign body into interpretation, not even into scientific interpretation. For the original goal of Scripture is to preach and to edify the Church, edification here being taken in its real sense of building up, not in a sentimental way. The Gospels are not a disinterested objective biography or history of Jesus. They are the proclamation and the demonstration of Jesus as the Christ. The New Testament epistles are not dogmatic treatises; their aim is always to edify and organize the Church by means of the word and by faith. The real aim of the New Testament writings is never therefore just narrative, but always the message. 'All that was written, was written for our hope, that through patience and the consolation of the Scriptures we might have edification' (Rom 15: 4). If exegesis does its work properly, it must give free rein to this aim of Scripture and make it efficacious. Otherwise it has not explained its text fully and in accordance with the reality.

These two aids to the hearing of the word, scientific exegesis on the one hand and the community of believers on the other, can only lead us to the point where each of us stands alone, confronted by the decision of faith. Each time the word of Scripture is made audible by expert exegesis and brought to us in the communion of the Church, the hearer is asked for a yes or no, to decide for faith or for unbelief. Scripture can only be accepted in the affirmation of the 'yes'. Such a consent, whatever be its nature, is in any case the presupposition for the understanding of all writings and human words. 'All things are known in so far as they are loved.' Still, the word of the New Testament comes to us with a demand made by no other text. It demands to be accepted as absolutely valid and final, and to be heard in a special way in faith: not because we have seen the intrinsic truth of the word, but because of God himself who reveals himself. Only when heard in faith can Scripture be truly understood. 'The word which is heard does not benefit, unless it finds faith in the hearers' (Heb 4:2).

Only in the assent of faith, which may indeed often cry out, 'Lord, I believe, help thou my unbelief' (Mk 9:24) can Scripture really be heard. The assent of faith, however, here implies that the formation of the mind and the giving of information must be purified and deepened by the formation of the conscience. It is clear that the reader of Scripture must first obey the call to repentance. The Gospel is the message of salvation and redemption. It can only be apprehended by one who knows and admits that he is guilty and in need of salvation. After repentance, and springing from it, there is demanded a life of effort according to the Gospel. So our Lord says, knowledge follows action. 'If any man does the will of God, he will know if my doctrine is from me or from God' (Jn 7: 17).

To hear and to explain Scripture thus becomes a science in the faith, a science of the hidden God, and theology in the true sense. Burdensome questions, historical or even theological, can and must remain. They must be borne because they belong to God's mysteries, and he is Lord of man, in judgment and in mercy, and is bound to give an account of himself to no one.

The sonnet of Rainer Maria Rilke, 'The Torso of Apollo', ends with the words:

> For there is no place that sees thee not,
> Thou must change thy life.

If that is true of seeing and understanding a statue, it is equally true of reading a book. It is most certainly true above all of reading the Bible and hearing the word. There is no place that does not *speak* to you, and speak to *you*. He who reads and hears the word must be ready to question himself and call himself into question, to let himself be called and exhorted. Only a reader who is ready to obey the ever new demands of the word may hope to hear the word.

Karl
Rahner, S.J.

EXEGESIS AND
DOGMATIC THEOLOGY

This essay is not wholly or even primarily concerned with the academic question of the relation of the two sciences, exegesis (and biblical theology) and dogmatics. It is rather inspired by the impression that within Catholic theology there obtains a certain estrangement between the representatives of these two disciplines. It appears to us that not a few representatives of these two fields of work in Catholic theology regard each other with a certain distrust, even exasperation. The dogmatic theologian seems at times to have the feeling that exegetes pay scant attention to the dogmatics to which the theologian is bound, and which pronounces upon matters which are the subject of exegesis (in the widest meaning of the word). Some exegetes, on the other hand, seem convinced that the theologians want to tie the Scripture scholar's hands in a way for which there is no objective justification, but simply because the theologians have not taken sufficient account of the progress Catholic exegesis has made in recent decades.

It is not our intention here to describe this strain more

31

closely or to prove it by documentation. Indeed, it is not something which has been clearly committed to writing in books and other printed testimony. The tension has rather been given expression in conversations, lectures and conferences, and in clerical gossip, which of course exists. To go into details would be to lose oneself in the jungle of personal clashes, sensibilities and polemics. This would be both pointless and fruitless.

If, however, the tension in question is not the spectre of a timorous imagination, and if it is not to give rise, in time, to serious damage both to science and to the Church, then it will be well to make a few basic statements about dogmatics and exegesis, soberly but very frankly. Covering up will not improve things or do away with them.

Some readers of this essay may get the impression, contrary to the facts and to the intention of the author, that German Catholic theology is in a bad state, by reason of real and personal difficulties, or that the author was seeking escape in publicity. That would be a mistake, but not a reason for omitting these considerations. Even correct and important disquisitions can be misunderstood.

We shall say nothing, directly or indirectly, of the shameful article written by A. Romeo against the professors of the Pontifical Biblical Institute, an article very damaging to the dignity and reputation of Catholic scholarship. (See A. Romeo, 'L'Enciclica "Divino Afflante Spiritu" e le "opiniones novae",' in *Divinitas*, 1960.) This article, however, also voiced unworthy suspicions against German exegetes in particular, denouncing the *brume nordiche*, the northern mists, which was its amiable way of mentioning German Catholic exegesis. It also apostrophized expressly certain German Catholic exegetes. And therefore we shall say just one thing in passing. German Catholic exegetes rightly feel that it is a hateful slander against their honour, their work and their attitude toward the Church when they are suspected of heresy and of sentiments contrary to the Church. Even a few hundred miles from Rome one can still be a good Catholic. We feel we can say that the Catholic theologians and the bishops, in solidarity with the German exegetes, reject decisively and unambiguously such massive and unqualified suspicions. But, as we have said, we do not wish to speak about this disgraceful episode.

We do intend to discuss, soberly and without polemics but on the grounds of basic principles, certain difficulties which have arisen. This does not mean that the situation of Catholic exegesis is alarming, or that those who call on the Church for bell, book and candle are finally in the right. On the other hand, it does not mean that one can simply forge ahead as if no problems or difficulties existed.

To-day, remarkably enough, these 'underground' problems which are the occasion of this essay are more concerned with the New Testament than with the Old. Thirty years ago things were different. We shall therefore attend principally to the questions which ought to be discussed more expressly and publicly between exegetes and theologians with regard to the New Testament. Much of what we say may sound like 'Father knows best', or the verdict of a self-appointed arbitrator. The reader must ask himself how such an impression could be avoided—except by not grasping the nettle. If he agrees that that would be even worse, he must simply put up with his disagreeable impressions. They are the inevitable by-products of a necessary process.

We shall say what we think without fear and in full freedom. We claim no more, it seems to us, than the right of a child in its father's house. The child need not be afraid of telling its parents, modestly and respectfully, what it thinks. This is merely the right which flows from the necessity of having such a thing as public opinion in the Church, lack of which has caused grave harm to Shepherd and flock, as Pius XII expressly declared when addressing the International Conference of Jurists in 1950. The division of the essay is simple. First we consider the exegetes and then the dogmatic theologians, ending up with some additional remarks.

To the Exegetes : from a Theologian

Dear brethren and revered colleagues. Permit me to think that you exegetes have not always enough consideration for us theologians and our dogmatics. Do not be offended if I pronounce rather massive verdicts. Anyone who feels that the cap does not fit need not wear it.

It seems to me however that you exegetes often forget that you are Catholic theologians. Of course you want to be, and you are. And I have not the least intention of voicing the unjust suspicion that you are ignorant or disdainful of the relationship between dogmatics and exegesis, faith and research, science and Church authority. But you are men, and sinners like the rest of men, including theologians. Hence it may happen that in your daily scientific labours you do not pay enough attention to these principles. In fact it often happens. You can forget, without denying it or rejecting it on principle, that you are engaged on a subject which is an intrinsic element of Catholic theology, and which must therefore observe all the rules which are in fact proper to Catholic theology.

Hence Catholic exegesis is a science of faith, not merely

philology and history of religions. It stands in a positive relationship to the faith and teaching authority of the Church. The doctrines and directives of this authority are not merely a negative norm for exegesis, a boundary not to be transgressed if one wishes to remain a Catholic. They are rather a positive intrinsic principle guiding research itself in scientific work, no matter how clearly one must keep in mind—of this we shall have more to say when addressing the theologians—what elements of exegesis and biblical theology are the result of purely philological and historical methods, and what are not. Nor can we here go into the concrete and exact detail of what we mean by saying that exegesis is strictly speaking a theological science, with all that that entails.

However, this can be easily grasped from a few external signs, as also the fact that you are not always conscious enough of it. I have the impression that you often go gaily and complacently about your work, as if it were pure philology and profane history. And when difficulties or problems arise which trouble dogmatic theology, or disturb the faith of your young theological students or lay people, you simply say that that is not your business, that is the affair of the theologians, let them deal with it. No, dear brothers. Theologians may well be given work to do by you, and they must not be vexed about it. But it is your most radically proper task to show the real compatibility of your results with Catholic dogma and, fundamentally at least, with official, if not defined, Church doctrine. You have not to force anything. You have not to be less than honest. But you have either to show such a compatibility, or if necessary, bring it about. For you are Catholic theologians. You have exactly the same responsibility with regard to Church doctrine and the belief of the simple faithful as the theologian has. Excuse my saying it, but one often has the impression that you are not always conscious enough of your responsibility, that you are almost maliciously, if mildly, glad when you can make difficulties, real or ostensible, for us theologians. One often has the impression that you greet the discovery of difficulties as the climax and proof of the authenticity and scientific quality of your research.

You must be critical, inexorably critical. You must not seek to arrange any dishonest reconciliations between the results of research and the doctrine of the Church. You may propose a problem and expound it sincerely where necessary. You need not have seen—in spite of all your efforts you may not yet see—how a clear, positive solution can be found which will harmonize Church doctrine, or what one takes to be such, with the real or ostensible results of your research. In such cases you need have no misgivings. But the climax of your research you must seek only in the accomplishment of your whole duty. And part of this, since you are Catholic exegetes, is the demonstration of the harmony between your results and Church doctrine. You must show how your results, of themselves, point on to Church doctrine as to their genuine expression. Of course not every exegete is bound to do this every time. Without specialization and division of labour, no one can get very far nowadays. But that such a demonstration is basically part of the exegete's task should show more often and clearly among you than seems to me to be the case.

And what happens then? When you relax and leave to us this task of bridge-building between exegesis and dogmatics, and when we poor theologians take it on ourselves and thereby take up exegesis, because a bridge has to go between *two* river-banks? Then—be honest!—you are the first to cry out that we theologians know nothing about exegesis, or that we practise a very cheap and truncated exegesis—a subject that we should leave alone. But who then is to accomplish the indispensable task?

You often give a very strange impression. You complain that we pay too little attention to Scripture, do too much scholastic theology and too little biblical. But when it is time to show where and how Catholic doctrine finds expression in Scripture or at least its ultimate basis, you begin to excuse yourselves and say that, with the best will in the world, you can find nowhere in Scripture to attach this or that Church doctrine. So with certain sacraments and some Mariological dogmas. You say that tradition and the teaching authority alone are responsible for them. But are you not responsible for the fact that many theologians seem to you to be indulging in extravagant and insubstantial speculation, since you suddenly renounce all Scriptural foundation for truths which belong also to your own Catholic faith? Whence is tradition supposed to have derived such truths? Being historians, you are the last who would believe in underground channels of tradition when you judge that something cannot be proved part of the public consciousness of the Church in the early centuries, either explicitly or implicitly. The teaching authority (magisterium) is the bearer of truths of faith, the bearer of a possible development, but not the material source of a truth of revelation.

In other words, suppose a doctrine has been declared as revealed by the later teaching authority and yet that doctrine is not explicitly taught in the writings of the Fathers accessible to us. Suppose it can be ascertained that the doctrine was not then 'orally' propounded—otherwise its absence from ancient literature is inexplicable. Then the

doctrine in question must be contained implicitly in Scripture. It is then the duty of the exegete also to offer his
contribution of biblical theology, so that the theologian,
with the help of unexceptionable exegesis, can show that
the doctrine was contained implicitly in Scripture. Is it not
therefore your duty to recognize the tasks that devolve on
you, and not pass them on too quickly to others? In many
cases, do you not take refuge too quickly behind the statement that the exegete has only to determine the immediate
sense of Scripture, and that the rest is not his trade?

Further—do not be offended—but I often get the impression that you are shy about stating expressly your principles—the exegetical, not just the dogmatic ones, but
such as derive immediately from exegetical work—and
showing that they agree with the principles of the teaching
authority. I know it is not easy. Under certain circumstances the exegete must say soberly that such and such
a declaration of the Biblical Commission of the beginning
of the twentieth century has either been superseded, or
is valid now only with certain qualifications. But you must
have the courage to do such 'dangerous' work, for it has
to be done and only you can do it, since we 'systematic
theologians', according to you, have no exact knowledge of
the individual problems of exegesis. And without such
knowledge the principles we speak of remain too general-
ized, too ambiguous, too vague, too unpractical to manage.
You have such principles, but you bury them in the detail
of your exegesis. Yet the exegetical layman, the theologian
for instance, asks himself in astonishment, when faced with
your work in detail, how this or that result stands with
regard to the inerrancy of Scripture or to Church canons
about the meaning of certain Scripture passages; how the
historical quality of a book can now be maintained; how

it is with the pseudonymity of a book; can such a 'false' attribution of authorship be accepted in principle even for the New Testament; how is one to do justice to the decrees of the Biblical Commission; and so on.

I am beginning to be rude. But permit me to make a somewhat malicious remark, because I admit it can also be made about theologians. If you knew your scholastic theology better, and if some practitioners of your great and sacred science did not look on scholasticism as a half-forgotten science, sunk so low that no one has practised it for centuries, your exegetical tasks would be easier, not harder. Take for instance the biblical doctrine of merit and the purely gratuitous nature of salvation. It seems to me that the exegetes could speak more clearly and in a more balanced way about it if the scholastic doctrine about the relation between grace and free-will were more distinctly before their minds, down to its last radical analysis. In such scholastic doctrine, biblical theology was actually being done, though in another set of concepts. Pardon me the following example, which is a mere passing reference to a distinguished work of exegesis, Ingo Hermann's *Kyrios und Pneuma* (Munich, 1961). If the author had not started from a doctrinal approach to the Trinity which seems to be very primitive, he would not have had to assert that no real doctrine of the Trinity can be found in St Paul. (And where, one might ask, is it to be found in the New Testament, if not even in St Paul? Presumably in whatever book one is not working on at the moment!) If one was clear about the scholastic teaching, which puts only a difference of relation between the persons, a distinction so fine as to be barely conceivable, one could find a similar distinction, though of course in other terms, in St Paul. Even for him 'Kyrios' and 'Pneuma' are not just two words for the self-same absolutely undifferentiated entity.

As a Catholic theologian, one may under certain circumstances have doubts about declarations of the magisterium with regard to doctrine, when it is not defined. But then one should say so clearly and give reasons. One should not get rid of the problem by simply passing it by in silence, and going on to other business. Often seeming contradictions, of more or less importance, which seem to occur as by-products of exegesis and appear to be in conflict with the teaching authority, are really only matters of terminology. And this often becomes apparent quite unexpectedly, where at first sight the matter seemed to be extremely dangerous. The exegete has, then, to keep the expressions of the teaching authority before his eyes, and to explain why there is no conflict between these declarations and his own results.

What is 'error', for instance, and what is not cannot be defined as easily as it might seem and as one takes for granted. The exegete may mean by 'error', such as he allows to be present somewhere in the New Testament, something that, put differently, covers a true and undeniable content. This no theologian must or will deny, any more than the Papal encyclicals which exclude all error in Scripture. The exegete gives this qualified meaning to the fact that the verse of Scripture which says that Abiathar (Mk 2 : 26) was high priest when David ate the loaves of proposition is in 'error'. But this it is only when the verse is read apart from its context, the literary form of the writing, and when it is detached from the frame of reference in which it was uttered and read in isolation—all of which the exegete has the right to do.

No real piece of knowledge, sobering though it may be

at first and productive of difficulties which must be sur-
mounted, can really be destructive. But it is well that the
laymen can really see that you are building up and not
pulling down, that you are promoting knowledge of the
life of Christ and not merely proving that historically
speaking there is much that cannot be known so exactly as
once was thought. You must make it clear that you do not
merely leave untouched the dogmatically undeniable facts
of the life, self-consciousness, and consciousness of mission
in Jesus, which for the dogmatic theologian are indispensable in Christology and Soteriology. You must also show
that you throw a clearer light on them and can sustain
them by methods of historical research. The theologian will
then understand more easily that you are right in not
regarding every single word of Jesus, even as given in the
Synoptic Gospels, as a sort of tape-recording or short-hand
record of what the historical Jesus said. He will understand
how you reckon—not merely theoretically and in general—
with the fact that theological interpretation was at work
in the transmission of the words of Jesus in the early
apostolic age, giving such words more precise meanings
and already modifying them to meet given circumstances
of the community.

I know that you are long since familiar with all this,
and for you it is no longer a problem. But everyone is not
like you. You must consider the 'weak in faith' and the
slow of understanding. You must take pains to make these
comprehend that you are building up and not pulling
down. You must teach your young theologians in such a
way that they suffer no harm to their faith and that they
do not think that their main job as curate will be to propound from the pulpit problems of exegesis which they
themselves only half understand, exaggerating them and

putting them before a public still less ready for them, to the astonishment and scandal of the faithful.

There is something else with which you might occupy yourselves more carefully than hitherto. It would do no harm to consider what are the *a priori* principles of dogma and fundamental theology (apologetics), prudently and exactly interpreted and grasped and nuanced in view of your own exegetical problems, and where they extend and with what obligations. You too have to observe them in your research into the life of Jesus, so that the Jesus of Gospel criticism may retain a historically demonstrable connexion with the Christ of faith. You have not to import the theology of the Council of Chalcedon into exegesis as such. But what the historical Jesus said of himself must, at least when taken in conjunction with the experience of Easter, be radically the same as what dogmatic Christology knows of Jesus.

It is quite permissible to define more precisely the literary forms of the miracle-stories in the Synoptics and St John. You may think that the general statement that these narratives are historical is too massive, especially when applied to single episodes. But it could be useful for you also, and in some cases a sort of emancipation, to consider more exactly the theory of miracles and what they essentially are, with regard to their reality and their recognizability. You must not give the impression that you think one could not know historically from the Gospels that Jesus worked miracles (especially that of the Resurrection) which are still significant to-day for the legitimation of his mission. If, as we may suppose, you have some idea of the dogmatic principles of fundamental theology, you will make it clear to your hearers that the Resurrection of Jesus is not just the object of faith, but also the foundation of faith in the Lord. No one will reproach you with having gravely transgressed your bounds if you tell your hearers how and why both are at the same time possible and correct.

Finally, it is unfair and hurtful both to you and to Protestant theologians, to reproach you with having taken over this or that item from Protestant exegesis. What does it prove, even if the statement is correct? Nothing at all. Protestant exegesis can in fact, as we should not have to emphasize, reach quite correct results. It is only right to adopt them when it is so. And when they are false and unacceptable? Then they must be rejected with indications of the objective reasons as to why they are false, not with the mere verdict that they are Protestant theology. Granted all this, however, ought you not avoid giving the impression, as you often do, that a Protestant thesis appears to you more probable simply because it grew out of Protestant exegesis and its original source was not Catholic? And must you not remember that Protestants often approach Scripture, not with an objective method based on exegesis, but with a philosophical *a priori* supposition?

To the Theologians : from a Colleague

I do not wish to tread on anyone's toes. I have to speak in general, where the only proper way would be to address myself individually to very different personalities. So I am going to address myself. Each of my revered colleagues in dogmatic theology should take as addressed to himself only as much as properly suits him. In the rest, he must have compassion on me, since I am lecturing myself.

So, dear friend, be honest. You know less about exegesis than is desirable. Being a theologian, you claim with justice that you have a right to do exegesis and biblical theology, and not merely rely on the results of specialists. After all, you say, your task as a theologian is to use every possible means to hear the word of God wherever it is uttered, and where better than in Sacred Scripture? But if so, you must do exegesis as it is done to-day, not the way it was done in the good old days. Or rather, not only in the old way. The exegesis you do in theology must also convince the specialists. They must grant you the right to put questions which do not concern them immediately as exegetes. You must envisage calmly the possibility that some exegetes will disagree with you on particular points, and will base their refusal on exegesis, not just on *their* exegesis. But if you are to talk to exegetes, you must really know how to manage their tools; you must really have felt their problems and the seriousness of their considerations. Otherwise you will find yourself soaring loftily above their problems on the wings of an over-simple distinction. Thus the theologian may be making things too easy for himself when he appeals to the *scientia incommunicabilis*, the non-communicable knowledge which Jesus still has, even though he declares that the Son does not know the day of the last judgment (Mk 13: 32). And if you are honest, you must admit that you have no explanation for such texts as, 'There are some of those standing by, that will not taste death, till they see the Kingdom of God coming with power' (Mk 9: 1), and, 'You will not finish all the cities of Israel, till the Son of Man comes' (Mt 10: 32). You must be glad if the exegetes find a solution, even though it appears to you too daring. And do not forget that such questions swim late into your ken, and are marginal in your system and in your estimation. They are much more weighty for the exegete, who meets them very early and so finds that they challenge him with a very different force, one that calls for a new orientation of his mind.

Be patient with the exegetes! To-day it is very difficult, given the immense vistas of a modern science and the complications of its methods, to understand enough of it to talk with one of its practitioners. We often think we know something about another science, but in fact it would have taken decades of working at it to understand. You must make yourself acquainted with the queries posed by exegetes, not in the summary 'objection' given in a scholastic manual, but in the long and careful studied monographs of the exegete. How many theologians can still do that? It is almost impossible, because the actual time and physical force are not at their disposal. So at least you must be cautious. Just do not quote a number from Denzinger's 'Church Documents' or a phrase from an Encyclical and say, 'that will not do!'

You complain that the exegete bothers too little about your criteria and norms and sources, and that he leaves all the trouble of bridge-building to you, as if it was not his business. But be careful not to do the same thing on your side! Do not forget that when dealing with Scripture, it is for you the inspired and infallible word of God, but the exegete as such must work from the point of view of 'fundamental theology' or apologetics. Having granted all we said about the theological nature of his exegesis, he is obliged to work on the New Testament as a historian, concerned with the foundations of the faith, precisely because he is a Catholic theologian who cannot start from the act of faith as if it were isolated and without foundation. If he did, he would be a poor theologian, because he would be denying that there is such a thing as the theology of the foundations of faith in a Catholic sense. Therefore he must investigate his sources, the New Testament, as if he were a historian. In this role he must recognize that the Synoptics are in substance historically reliable sources. It is true, of course, that having said that they are reliable sources for the life of Christ, we are still far from having described the Synoptic type of literature exactly enough to lay the ground for a verdict on the real value of any particular statement. The statement may read to-day, at first sight, like a historical item. But it may not be so in terms of modern historical writing.

The main thing is this: The exegete must be able to work on the New Testament and its transmission, and be able to prescind, methodologically, from the inspiration and inerrancy of Scripture. He has thus the right and the duty, even while maintaining, as a profane historian, the historicity of the substance of the Synoptics, not to accept *a priori* every statement of Scripture as equally certain in history. If he did so he would, as far as methodology is concerned, have switched from fundamental theology to dogmatics. This would not be an advantage, but a mistake. Even where—and this is probably by no means the case everywhere—a Synoptic evangelist makes a statement which he himself wishes to be taken as historical, the exegete, the scholar engaged on research into the life of Jesus, is not bound to declare that every such statement has the same sure and certain historical value. When it is absolutely certain that the evangelist intends to assert something as an historical event in our modern sense, the exegete working from the point of view of fundamental theology certainly may not say, 'the evangelist is surely wrong here'. But neither is he obliged to affirm that the evangelist is surely right.

We theologians think that we must maintain that Jesus

had direct vision of God in his earthly life, because it is the obligatory, though not defined, doctrine of the recent popes since Benedict XV. Since this is so, you as a theologian are bound to show the exegete—really, and not merely by juggling with concepts—how this doctrine is compatible with the impression the exegete gains from the Synoptic Gospels about the historical Jesus. You must show more clearly than you usually manage to do that the cares of your colleague the exegete are not entirely unknown to you, that you have some practice in his methods and know how to appreciate his results.

You have an easier task than your colleague, who works on the foundations of the faith. You can take every word of Scripture from the start as equally inspired and infallible, and you can use it as a valid proof in your dogmatics. You need not ask yourself exactly where it comes from. You can be indifferent to whether it is, as it stands, a historically certain word of Jesus, or whether it has already been modified by the theology of the community and of the New Testament writers. You need not concern yourself directly with whether it is part of the primitive data of revelation, or whether it is the theology of the Apostles, arrived at by deduction—correctly of course and infallibly. You can proceed that way though, be it said in passing, that is not really the ideal even of the dogmatic method, because the exact interpretation of a text can depend on the answers to the questions with which textual criticism and history of the development of tradition must busy themselves. But would it do any harm if, when giving a dogmatic proof of the Trinity from Scripture, you made it clear that you knew the questions which the historian asks about the final apostolic mission (Mt 28: 16–20)? And since you may, there being no absolute dogmatic barrier to it, can you not show that you are reckoning calmly with the fact that the trinitarian formula found there on the lips of Jesus may have been worked out to some extent by the theology of the community?

There could be many problems intrinsic to dogmatics as such which the theologian could and should raise, because the answers to them would be really liberating for the exegete and a lightening of his burden. In the course of dogmatic theology, for instance, we ask how exactly the appearances of the Risen Lord are to be thought of with regard to the essence of the matter. After all, and this is most important, he no longer belongs at all to the world of our experience and phenomena. To have had experience therefore of the Risen Lord must be entirely different from a meeting with Lazarus raised from the dead. The consequence would be perhaps that the variations in the accounts of the apparitions, which are found in the story of Easter, are only to be expected in the nature of things, and that there is no need of any artificial touching-up to harmonize them.

Again, when dealing with the intrinsic difficulties of the Trinity and of Christology, we theologians could perhaps make many things clear from the start which would help the biblical theologian to understand that his subject and scholastic theology are really expounding the same reality. For instance, we could probably expound the doctrine without simply repeating the formulations of 'person' and 'nature'. We could well show that the inner-trinitarian process and the mission of the Son and Spirit for the work of redemption are so connected that the immanent processions have already been spoken of when the mission *ad extra* has been correctly presented, as is done in Scripture. Basing ourselves on an existentialist ontology, we

could develop a 'Christology of Ascent', of confrontation
with the man Jesus, which would be closer to the point of
view of the Synoptics and the Acts than if we merely
present Christology as the descent of the Lord to take on
human nature.

There is also the doctrine of the immediate vision of
God possessed by Jesus' soul in his earthly life. In itself
the vision is a basic condition undifferentiated in consciousness (see the last essay in this book). A truly metaphysical understanding of the doctrine could be so presented that the exegete could see that the scholastic
analysis does not really deprive him of his right to note
authentic growth, real dependence on the religious milieu,
and unexpected crises in the life of Jesus. Would it not be
worthwhile, for instance, to ask oneself whether in certain
circumstances a certain kind of ignorance could not be
the more perfect thing, in contrast to knowledge? Take the
matter of the freedom of a creature. Jesus had such freedom and used it. He was truly one who adored, and truly
one who obeyed the incomprehensible will of the Father.
Is it not of the essence of such freedom that in the act of
decision one marches into the wide-open unknown, which
one only 'knows' as it really is when one accepts it lovingly
as the unknown?

Why do we theologians not reckon more clearly with the
fact, which is psychologically and existentially obvious,
that 'to know' is not an univocal concept? That a man can
have several very different types of knowledge which
cannot be translated from one type to another? Why not
admit that one can really know something in a certain
way, while the very same thing, even as it is in itself, may
remain unknown in another way? If one is radically one
with God, then in him one knows 'everything', as pro-

4

foundly as the divine reality is experienced. That does not mean that one must know it immediately, or wish to know it, in that dimension of the human spirit in which one is conscious of articulate, express individual items of knowledge. Such a dimension of knowledge might render impossible or disturb under certain circumstances that silent one-ness with the one real truth. Why then should we theologians forbid the exegete to say, in a true sense (which of course does not coincide with the whole reality of Jesus), that there were many things which Jesus did not know? After all, he said so himself (Mk 13:32), and we have no real reason to play about with the meaning of his words with our distinctions.

Very often we have quite correct principles in theology which are to some extent metaphysical ones. But we do not notice how wide and spacious they are and how much can be fitted into them. So we do not make it clear enough to the exegete who is working from facts, that he may start calmly and without embarrassment from the results of his research into the life of Jesus and find a really living man, with a history which he is not obliged to pass by. And still he will know that his hands have touched the Word which became flesh! We start from the silent presupposition that the Resurrection is a great miracle, which legitimates the mission of Jesus. And we suppose that if God had willed it, this miracle could have been worked on any other man also. We suppose that such a resurrection could be independent of the 'first-born' Son of Man and his resurrection, and that it could take the form, not of a renewed earthly life like Lazarus', but of the total and final fulfilment of resurrection. But is such a supposition clearly and actually true? Is there not another way of looking at things, deeper and more exact? The onset of absolute salvation, which is not just a stage in the process but the definitive, unsurpassable salvation of God in person, which is manifested and effected in the Resurrection—is this not necessarily the Son of God in the sense of the Christology of Chalcedon?

A 'functional' Christology asks not what are the natures of Christ, but what he means for us and what he does for us. May one not suspect all the same that it contains the traditional 'ontological' Christology, if it is thought out radically enough? Completed in such a way, could not this 'functional' Christology, while preserving its proper character, open up the faith to many, who for fear of the 'mythology' which they wrongly suspect to be present, would otherwise never find the way to the faith? The official theology of the Church is not monophysite. But monophysite misapprehensions have often affected the faith of individual Christians, who see the 'human nature' of the Word as scarcely more than a uniform or a puppet for the Godhead, something that only looks towards us, but does not also look toward God in the freedom of dialogue? Could not such attitudes also be corrected by a truly 'functional' theology? And from this same standpoint, could one not see better how a 'Christology of the Resurrection', which makes little apparent effort to appeal to Jesus' self-designation in his earthly life to explain his nature, but looks simply to the Resurrection, need not be simply false?

To-day, even among Catholic exegetes, there is a tendency to view a great many things only in the light of the Resurrection, and to consider as already interpreted in the light of the Resurrection what is narrated about the words and deeds of Jesus' earthly life. Should there not be more sympathy for this approach, even though it should be used with caution, and not all statements of Jesus about his nature in his historical life which imply his ontological Sonship of God may be contested. Indeed, there is no historical reason to contest them, provided that one does not think that such forms of self-designation must more or less talk in terms of the immediate 'communication of idioms' or an almost Chalcedonian set of concepts.

There is the question of original sin in the New Testament. If we theologians started our treatise by insisting on the merely analogical nature of the sin in the good, established scholastic doctrine, we could make it clear that man can as it were 'ratify' original sin by his personal sin. Then, centuries after Erasmus, our exegetes would not have to think that they must defend St Augustine's explanation of the '*in quo*' (i.e. in Adam) of Romans 5: 12. And it could have been recognized earlier that possibly Romans 5: 12, according to the simple sense of the words, speaks of the sinning of the individual man; which does not mean that this chapter says nothing of original sin, rightly understood.

Probably the most important thing for us theologians, however, if we are to do justice to the exegetes, is to understand that to call a narrative 'historical' is in many cases too loose a way of talking, even where it is correct. The predicate 'historical narrative' when applied to the New Testament and within this to the Synoptic Gospels, does not mean, for instance, that the discourses of Jesus are more or less tape-recordings, abbreviated at the most by omissions. It is almost embarrassing as a dogmatic theologian to say this expressly once again. But our work in dogmatics constantly inclines us toward a mentality that thinks this way, even though—at least in theory—we have long since recognized that it is false. We cite the words of

Jesus for our proofs, and so slip again and again very easily into the attitude that the very words we quote must have been exactly so on the lips of Jesus, just as if we had been there and heard them. But in the New Testament there is no such type of historical literature as would guarantee that we have such a record. This fact must be seriously taken into account, for it can be demonstrated by many examples, and must be allowed for methodologically, even where a comparison of the Synoptics does not show it up clearly. As regards the exegetes, this is their daily bread. As regards the theologians, it is a sort of abstract and fleeting concession, granted incidentally. No wonder we only understand each other with difficulty.

It would however be wrong to think that everything goes by the board and that nothing remains secure historically, even if we begin by accepting coolly and courageously the fact that even in the Synoptic Gospels the words of Jesus are not just simply recorded. They have been altered in oral transmission; they have been clarified in the interests of theology; they have been given glosses which are not expressly signalled; they have been given plastic and dramatic turns. Historical criticism must take this into account. More precisely still: the individual elements of the Gospels have had a pre-history of one sort or another before they ultimately reached the Gospel books. Form-criticism has rightly made us aware of that. Therefore we must be prepared to recognize that the individual items, when compared with one another, do not all belong to the same literary type of history. Hence, from the point of view of fundamental theology and historical criticism, it is not so certain that Jesus was in Egypt as that he was crucified in Jerusalem. This does not undermine the authority of the narrative. Because of its very nature, the narrative admits of such questioning. It makes no claim to be a painstaking report, ready for the files of the police, of 'just' what historically happened and could have been observed by anybody.

This is a possibility to be reckoned with. But of course the question of where, how, when and to what extent something of the sort really intervened is not thereby answered with regard to the individual narratives of the words and deeds of Jesus. To ascertain this in particular cases, within the boundaries of the possible, is the business of a proper historical criticism of the New Testament. Such criticism often renders the task of the dogmatic theologian more difficult, but in many cases it makes it easier. Take for instance the parenthesis of Matthew 5:32, 'Everyone who divorces his wife (apart from the case of fornication) causes her to commit adultery'. If the exception can be regarded as a gloss added by the casuistry of the community, the theologian is better off than if the exception had been made directly by Jesus himself. It is quite possible that texts which cause such difficulties for theologians as Mark 9:1 and Matthew 10:23, already mentioned, may lose their sting if one may say with the historical critics that Jesus could not simply have uttered them as they stand, that is with such temporal precisions, or at least with what appear to be such. Of course, in view of the inerrancy and inspiration of Scripture, the texts are not merely to be set aside, and all this makes the work of theologian and exegete more difficult. But that is not a proof that one could save trouble by using simpler principles.

As we have already said, it is not true that in the end no one knows what really happened. There is much that we cannot know exactly. But historically we can know enough to hold on to those fundamental data of apologetics which are the basis of the doctrine of the Church with regard to the person and the work of Jesus. And we can have true historical certainty, no matter how little that may be interchangeable with metaphysical certainty or the certainty of faith, and no matter how hard it is to speculate and analyse when and why such knowledge, in spite of its various levels and difficulties, can indeed be called certain'. When the layman in history is confronted with the painstaking deliberations of the scholar about what exactly happened to Caesar in Gaul, his head may perhaps begin to spin. He gets the impression that finally one does not even know whether Caesar was ever in Gaul. Such historical vertigo is understandable, but it is not thereby justifiable.

The same thing can happen with the work of the exegete, provided of course that he has been working conscientiously and not making his chief business the destruction of ostensible certainties, and provided also that he retains the character of a believing theologian even while doing his work of exegesis, an attitude—though of course belief should not enter as an objective norm into fundamental theology as such—which will give him a better chance of working well on history than if he were blind to what is announced in the New Testament, the miracle of the grace of God in Jesus Christ. But why should we theologians not credit our exegetes with such attitudes? We are not bound to accept every particular item of their work with blind confidence in the experts. We have the right and the duty to do exegesis ourselves, as well as we can, as far as we wish, and calmly check the findings of the exegetes. But we have no right to succumb to *our* temptation and behave (mostly only in silence) as if their method itself were to be greeted with contradiction.

It is quite another question to ask what significance the correct and mature findings of exegesis may have for preaching, teaching and religious edification. From the pulpit, the preacher rightly starts, as is his duty, from the sacredness of the book, which the exegete working from the point of view of fundamental theology cannot do in the same way. The principles at work therefore in a sermon from the pulpit are different from those in a lecture of a professor in the exegetical seminar. There is therefore no place in the pulpit for much of what the exegete does in fundamental theology, even though the faithful have the right to hear nothing from the pulpit which is contrary to the assured results of exegetical research. In what measure the faithful are to be introduced to the problems of such research will depend on the age and the culture of each group. It is to be done by lectures and articles rather than by the Sunday sermon. It must always be remembered, however, that preaching is the proclamation of the word of God and serves the building up of the faithful.

Some Additional Considerations

Theologians and exegetes must remember that they are not the masters but the servants of the teaching office, which Christ entrusted to St Peter and the Apostles, not to the professors. But the professors know, with Hegel, that God has so constituted the world that the master needs the servant, and thus in spite of his superiority, is also dependent on him.

These servants of the teaching office need the confidence of this authority, and free room to work in with confidence, for without it they cannot perform their modest but necessary task.

The ecclesiastical sciences, and above all exegesis, have more to do to-day than to fulfil the scientific tasks which interest scholars. They must be front-line fighters for the faith and the Church. They must make the possibility of faith clear to modern man. They must instruct, strengthen and console the intellectual. The intellectual is the spiritual child of positivist history and the natural sciences, a terribly sober, cautious and disappointed man: a man who suffers from the distance and the silence of God, as now he feels it. This is the man the Church has to deal with. For he is precisely the man of to-day and to-morrow. It would be simpler to restrict the preaching of the faith to other men, who come from different spiritual levels of society, who 'believe' easily, simple humble men who have not really been affected by the mental climate of our times. Their religion is strengthened by social bonds. They put intellectual problems aside for various reasons, or resolve them privately in a very 'uncatholic' way. They let nothing disturb their official 'churchmanship'.

But the Church must occupy itself with the real intellectual of to-day, and not leave him abandoned in his own sort of need of faith and his own sort of willingness to believe. He who does not admit this need of faith misunderstands the real problems of our times. Such a need is there, and ecclesiastical sciences have not to go in for inbreeding but must think of the men of to-day. But if theology is to do this, it cannot by-pass difficult and dangerous questions. It must look for solutions that are novel and untested, because it is simply impossible to go on repeating the good old truths that have been tried and tested. They must at the very least be skilfully re-formulated in the interests of pedagogy and psychology.

It may well be that the ultimate problems of faith are not decided on the field of individual questions and problems of theology. But the non-theological intellectual of to-day has the impression that there is a multitude of such questions to-day that are not being answered, that there is no honest and simple answer, that they are being skirted, that honest discussion is forbidden. Taken as a whole, such unanswered questions generate a situation and a mental atmosphere which—while the ultimate basic decisions of life are still felt as burdensome—can be deadly for the faith of modern man. He must have a clear and intelligible answer from the ecclesiastical sciences to the following questions: What about evolution? What has the Church really to say to the whole history of religions? What about the destiny of the countless men who are non-Christians? Why do we seem nowadays to have so few miracles, while the ancient books tell us so many that are more splendid and convincing? How is it with the immortality of the soul and the proofs for it? There are endless questions of this sort. Sometimes they are not put expressly, out of weariness or out of fear—fear for the little bit of faith that has still survived and that one wishes to save! But in any case they form the mental atmosphere in which the intellectuals of to-day, whose number is constantly growing, are living in fact and inescapably. Among such questions belong also the exegetical and theological problems of the Bible: the historical reliability of Scripture, including the New Testament, the credibility of the miracles narrated in it, the historical recognizability of the Resurrection, the relation of the teaching of Jesus to the theology and practices of his milieu. If exegesis tried to avoid these and the many similar questions which arise, it would be betraying its duty. Such questions are difficult and 'dangerous'.

The Church has always admitted that there are different schools of theology with different outlooks, indeed, that there should be. From the point of view of pure logic, the conflicting principles of these schools could under certain circumstances be dangerous to the faith, even objectively. Two assertions from conflicting schools cannot be true from the same stand-point at the same time. But this danger to the faith has never been felt subjectively. And rightly so. Everyone knows that, historically, each of the conflicting schools maintained whole-heartedly the basic principles which are to be maintained in such open questions, and wished to maintain them. The theologians could therefore be left to their debate without any misgivings. The Church did not intervene, but left room for freedom, to the benefit of theology.

In the questions posed to theology to-day, it is inevitable that solutions should be weighed and tested whose compatibility with the authentic doctrine of the Church is not at once obvious and clearly ascertainable. Such questions cannot always get an answer whose 'safety' is beyond doubt and debate. It may be a very long time before it can be seen that such an answer is unexceptionable from the point of view of the Church. The place for discussing such problems is primarily among experts, as far as possible, before they are made accessible to a wider public. This is an excellent principle, but one which is not always practicable even with the best will in the world. For there are many questions not yet clarified and settled by the expert theologians, which are still the questions debated among modern men and not just the private affair of the theologians.

We cannot console these men by saying, 'later, later, wait till expert opinion is formed, till there is an acceptable solution which will be acknowledged by all theologians and the teaching authority'. We must answer now; we must speak in such a way that even the layman can hear an answer to his questions. The answer may be wrong, as may be proved later. It may fall short of the mark. It may, in spite of the good will of the theologian, be objectively irreconcilable with the certain principles of the teaching authority. It may be correct and timely, and still raise the question of the revision of certain official—but not defined—declarations, the need for which has often been accepted in the past. It may be that correct views simply need a period of incubation in Church teaching, till 'people' are used to them, and their agreement with the ancient faith of the Church has been experienced existentially and sentimentally. The official teaching authority of the Church has certain rights and duties here. It must supervize the process of groping and seeking, the serious discussion on which something really depends. It must check all wild growths and bar the way, as soon as possible, to all developments which are surely heading for heresy. This every Catholic theologian takes for granted. Nor does he think that every measure taken by the teaching authority is wrong or unjust simply because it is hard and painful for some theologians.

But it is not true that this time of questioning, of discussion and of seeking can simply be skipped, and replaced once and for all by decisions of the teaching office. This teaching office, according to Catholic doctrine, is the only authority which can promulgate a decision which will be binding in conscience in matters of theology, even on experts. But it is not an isolated authority which can, on its own, clarify open questions. For this it needs the discussion, the reflexions of the theologians. Theologians are not just poisonous but pretty flowers, or a debating society which meets for its own amusement. They have a function that is valuable in itself and indeed irreplaceable; nor is this factor eliminated by the possible union of Church superior and scientific authority in one person. Theologians are necessary in the Church. They must debate and they must discuss the problems of their day, and in these discussions even untried, dangerous and perhaps finally impracticable and un-Catholic opinions (as may eventually appear) must be risked.

This is not the green light for wild opinions, and for notions which every sane theologian must recognize as impossible from the start. There should be no need to insist on this. True, from the point of view of scientific theory, it is also clear and must be stated without apology that there is no such thing as a formal principle whereby we may draw the line at once and unwaveringly between freely debatable questions, and opinions which are to be rejected out of hand. It remains then that both sides must risk a dangerous decision, according to the best of their knowledge and as their conscience tells them. Church authority can brake or forbid at first an opinion which may appear later as fitting matter for discussion. A theologian may maintain that a certain opinion is open to discussion, when in reality it is not from the start, and when it justly evokes immediate contradiction on the part of the teaching authority. These inadequacies come with the fact that man and the Church are finite and creatures. Against them there is only one remedy, humility, patience and love.

What has been said in these pages is really self-evident. It was not put forward because another view could be seriously held, but because certain consequences which are perhaps less obvious have to be deduced from it. And these consequences seem to us both correct and important. Let us take the case of theologians who are discussing a delicate question raised by to-day's exegesis. The theologian and exegete may be obliged to intervene in the discussion by affirming that his colleague's opinion is not compatible with some principle laid down by the official teaching authority of the Catholic Church. This verdict may be true or false, but it should be possible to give it. One cannot simply say that the man holding a questionable opinion has himself the instruments for recognizing such a discrepancy. If that were so, then the theologian in question, being a Catholic, would never have put forward the opinion. No, it is quite possible that a theologian, in all sincerity, can advance an opinion which is objectively to be challenged, from the point of view of theology and the Church. And he need not notice this at once.

Let us envisage now a theologian who feels obliged to use these legitimate weapons against a colleague. If he had to foresee that his challenge would at once put the other within range of ecclesiastical censure or of dismissal from his teaching chair, he would probably avoid proceeding in this just and necessary way, and thereby do harm. He would remain silent, or talk around the subject, or confine his comments to the class-room. The truth would not be served, and the frank brotherly openness which should reign among Catholic theologians would suffer damage. It is no excuse to say that the other has only himself to blame when his opinions draw the fire of the ecclesiastical authorities. For the colleague who thinks of challenging him can be sincerely convinced of the high theological quality of his opponent, of the stimulating value of the unacceptable opinion, of the blamelessness of the other's ecclesiastical orthodoxy. He could therefore seriously think that his opponent should escape ecclesiastical censure, though he himself entirely rejects the other's view and is ready to combat it. But if he has the impression that his No to such an opinion would bring the other within danger of censure, he would shrink from putting forward his opinion in the form stated above. He would not wish to be guilty of bringing down a censure on another. That is understandable and quite honourable.

But such silence or soft-pedalling would in fact do harm. It would hinder the necessary debate, and in certain circumstances it would mean abandoning the necessary defence of Catholic doctrine, for which the theologian is to some extent responsible. It would force the Church authorities to take on a function which the theologian himself should exercise. It would force theological discussion to abandon the publicity of books and periodicals and take up a sort of underground warfare carried on only by word of mouth.

We do not of course suggest that the ecclesiastical authorities would simply accept, sight unseen, the verdict of one theologian on another, or that they would be taking unjust and unnecessary measures when they proceeded to a censure. But it cannot be maintained on the other hand that unjust or unnecessary procedures are unthinkable or that they have never been used. But if hasty, objectively unjust or over-severe measures, which do harm to the great reality they try to serve, are not unthinkable in such matters, then the theologian may well fear their coming. If he thought they could come relatively easily, he would try to avoid bringing them down upon a colleague. Discussion would be lamed, and problems would remain unsolved.

At the most, a censure can bar the way to a false route. It does not thereby open up the right way.

Since this is so, one may well think that official censures (correct and objective in themselves, not merely possible but necessary) should be applied only rarely and with caution, after the whole context has been weighed and all extenuating circumstances, where a theologian has expressed an opinion in free discussion because he felt it his honourable duty as professor. Otherwise the necessary function which theological discussion has in the Church will be thrown out of gear, to the detriment of true doctrine, not to its gain. Negative official measures should not be taken on the basis of the silent presupposition that every false doctrine not expressly forbidden by the Church will range unchecked in all directions: as if they could not be stopped by purely theological means, namely by clarification of the question.

If censures follow too often and too quickly, the view would arise spontaneously among theologians, contrary to the intention of the authorities, that an opinion was compatible with the Catholic faith simply because it was not immediately combatted by the teaching authority. If in a particular case the censure does not follow, simply because it cannot always happen, then the theologian would be less ready than ever to trust himself when expressing the opposite opinion. He would think that his own rejection of the opinion must be false, because otherwise the ecclesiastical authorities would have intervened. Thus the authorities would be forced to act more quickly than ever, to avoid giving the impression that this or that opinion was tolerable from the Catholic point of view. The necessary function of the theologian would be paralysed. Under the silent presupposition that any declaration of the teaching authority, which is not a definition, can in the end be corrected, the situation becomes more confused than ever. One theologian is silent because he is afraid of being censured, another, because he does not wish to bring down a censure on a third. And when the teaching authority speaks, its declaration will be accepted not as doctrinal legislation, but as a purely disciplinary measure, to be silently evaded where possible.

This essay was not written to describe an alarming situation which is actually in existence, but to give an analysis of the possible mechanics of a mentality which could go into action if the ecclesiastical authorities had too little confidence in the positive results of debate among theologians, and hence thought that they had to intervene in the debate at the earliest possible moment.

Anton
Vögtle

PROGRESS AND PROBLEMS IN NEW TESTAMENT EXEGESIS

The two Testaments which make up Sacred Scripture are, even up to the present day, still judged very differently in many circles. The Old Testament has long been known to be a collection of writings of various types, which demand historical and literary research on a high level. Each book and group of writings must be set against its particular age and milieu; its sources and its literary forms must be examined, if the real assertions of the author are to be properly grasped. Every student at matriculation level knows this as a matter of course. So the Old Testament enjoys the privilege, in general estimation, that not everything in it must be taken and 'believed' as it stands—indeed, far from it! And no one thinks there is anything very strange when Old Testament exegesis speaks of a large number of unresolved problems, which up to now have remained insoluble.

The same cannot be said of the New Testament which is, to be sure, a later book. Some hesitations are allowed, of course. The Apocalypse, with its strange symbols is a difficult work, but after all, it is not so important. The epistles, especially those of St Paul, may indeed provide room for learned research and speculation, because they soar so often to the heights of theology. But in any case, these epistles were all written by the Apostles whose names they bear, and stand in the light of the long-familiar Church history, so beautifully presented by St Luke in the Acts of the Apostles. Without shadow of doubt, finally, the Gospels, these copious narratives of the life and work of the Saviour, are valued as exemplary models of unsurpassable simplicity and directness, which every child can understand exactly as does the greatest scholar. It is taken for granted that everything without exception is and must be intended as it stands. Everything must have happened and been said, seen and heard, exactly as can be read in each of the four Gospels, and as far as possible in the sequence there given. If it were not exactly so, what would become of inspiration and inerrancy? That New Testament research presents, in its own field, the same questions and historical problems as the Old, is something that has as yet scarcely penetrated the general consciousness.

Karl Rahner took this situation as the occasion for his opening remarks, a very instructive address to his colleagues in theology and exegesis, in which he said: 'To-day, remarkably enough, these "underground" problems which are the occasion of this essay are more concerned with the New Testament than with the Old. Thirty years ago things were different' (see above, page 33). And in fact, it is incontestable that Catholic New Testament research has gone through a certain delayed development in the last thirty years. During this period, it too began to make its voice heard in systematic theology, bringing essential acquisitions, but also real questions and problems. Thus a force came into play which was felt as stimulating, stirring and exciting, even in many ways evolutionary. This will not be particularly surprising, if we look at the place of exegesis in theology, and the main factors in its recent development. It is now both a theological and historical discipline, fully conscious of its dual role.

The High Theological Relevance of the New Testament

Allow me to begin with something obvious, for the sake of its importance. The particular gravity of the findings, the open questions, and difficulties of New Testament exegesis lies basically in their subject-matter. The New Testament books happen to be, from the purely historical view-point, the earliest written documents of the revelation of Christ, and of the life and doctrine of the Church, the Church of the first century. They deal with the final closing of revelation, with the Finisher and fulfilment of the Old Testament prophecies given in act and in word, and with the final order of salvation of the New Covenant. They narrate many miracles, which were or will be performed by Jesus, or by God on his person. Some of these stand in the Creed of the Church as central salvific events and truths. At every step, they confront the reader with the basic and decisive questions: the person of the bringer of revelation and redemption, his relation to God 'the Father' and to the Spirit, his work of salvation which embraces past, present, and future. They present the question of the foundation and constitution of the Church, its initial realization, its growth into the Church of the Gentiles, its understanding of Christ and salvation, its sacramental activity and so on.

In all this, the exegete, precisely because he is a Catholic student of the New Testament, must put very concrete questions to the text. For instance, with regard to the last point, he must ask: What can we know about the number of sacraments instituted by Christ and administered from the beginning? Who were the valid ministers? In the churches founded by St Paul, for instance, and specifically, say, in Corinth, who was charged with the celebration of the Eucharist and was responsible for it? What happened to the baptized who committed sin—as presumably they did ever since people were baptized? Clearly, to be able to answer these and dozens of similar questions from the pages of the New Testament is of immediate interest and importance for the doctrine and practice of the Church in later times and at the present day. The New Testament deals with the final revelation, that is, the order of salvation now valid. Hence many results and problems arising from the texts gain an imperiously greater actuality than similar examples from the Old Testament.

The words of the Risen Lord in his many mandates to his disciples, both in the Gospels and in the Acts, are saturated with problems. To select but one by way of example, we note that the command to baptize in Matthew 28:19 is couched in a trinitarian formla. To-day the great majority, even of Catholic exegetes, take it that here we must see 'a definite step in the evolution of the Christian profession of faith at baptism' (J. Schmid, *Das Evangelium nach Matthäus*, 1959). The Epistles of St Paul, like the Acts of the Apostles, know baptism only in, or unto, the name of Jesus. In the whole New Testament, the fully developed formula which unmistakably surpasses all other trinitarian elements and initial statements, especially in St Paul and St John, is found only in Matthew 28:19. It is therefore held that the formula put on the lips of the

Risen Lord in Matthew 28 : 19 does not represent the starting-point of the post-Easter proclamation of the Trinity, but to some extent its climax. It is the final result of the efforts of the primitive Church at a conceptual grasp of the Trinity. A development in the opposite direction is hardly conceivable. Certainly, the dogmatic truth is unimpaired. And in addition, baptism 'in the name of Jesus' implied objectively from the beginning the reference to the Trinity.

The dogmatic theologian, who thinks he must take this explanation into account, will still know how to appreciate Matthew 28 : 19 as the *locus classicus* of his historical proof and of his proof from Scripture. He will see it as the expression of the faith of the Church, or of a province of the Church, at the end of the apostolic generation. None the less, everyone will admit that it was quite a different thing when a professor of the Old Testament made the same kind of statement thirty years ago. If he remarked that some legal ordinance of the Pentateuch was not from the time of Moses, but reflected a later development, we were not very deeply concerned, because in any case Christ had abolished such laws. It was something else again to hear that the trinitarian formula of Matthew 28 : 19 was not uttered by the Risen Lord himself.

Let us take another example. How far, and in what sense, according to the statements of Jesus and the primitive Church, will our earth and indeed the whole universe be affected by the full manifestation of the Reign of God, when 'this world' is succeeded by the 'world to come'? Where does imagery cease and an event begin which affects the physical world? Exegetes who 'de-mythize' the New Testament answer the question very simply, but undoubtedly far too simply. But is it enough to say with many

Catholic exegetes that the events described in Mark 13:24 f. and in the parallels would not touch the earth at all and would not imply any real disturbance of the universe, of space above the earth? Can we say that they only give a vivid picture of the immense power of the coming of the Son of Man, so that we may speak of the 'end of history' but not of the 'end of the world'? There remain similar passages in other contexts which still need to be explained (especially 1 Cor 7:31, Rom 8:20 ff., Mt 19:28, Heb 12:26 f., 2 Pt 3:10–13, Ap 21:1–5).

Is there an idea and a statement common to all these? Some say that these images merely bring out God's sovereign dominion over the world, but make no assertion about the fate of the universe; or that only the earth and its atmosphere will be involved in the 'new creation' at the end of time. But does this really give the meaning of the inspired authors, which is what really matters? 'Heaven' in the sentence, 'the first heaven and the first earth passed away' (Ap 21:1), can only mean in biblical cosmology the universe beyond the region of earth, though its magnitude was not then suspected. The expression, 'first creation', of Apocalypse 21:4 confirms this unambiguously. If so, does not the final revelation of the Kingdom of God also mean the 'End', the passing away of the whole universe, a new creation in which the world is transformed and brought to its perfection?

The question of the whole universe being involved in the last act of Redemption could be not without importance under certain circumstances. Many theologians envisage the possibility that one day men-like beings may be discovered on other planets, and meet it with the explanation which is not of itself without plausibility: that the process of salvation established for the race of Adam and which is completed by the events of the second coming of Christ, would not be valid for another world of men. They would come under another dispensation. However, all we wish to draw from this example is that as regards the 'End' of the world and of mankind, the exegete is far worse off than when explaining the account of creation in the Book of Genesis with regard to the absolute beginning of the world. The Old Testament scholar has relatively little difficulty in making a clear and convincing cut between the imagery and the truths there asserted. He can happily leave the whole 'how' to natural science which, we may add, envisages an end to the world according to scientific laws, but does not discuss its transformation.

The Origin of the Books of the New Testament: the World of the Past

There is a second point which must not be entirely over-looked. The persons who speak in the New Testament, like the authors of the different books themselves, belong to a past world. Their way of thinking, imagining and express-ing themselves is very different from ours. The immediate surroundings in which Jesus and his Apostles worked is not just the world of the Old Testament. It is also the changing and developing world of 'Judaism', with its many facets, and also the pagan world of Hellenism. The exegete is constantly oppressed by the feeling that he knows too little of this world with its many levels, that he cannot reconstruct it well enough to be able to expound his text securely in all its bearings, its possible depths of meaning, and in all its details. And there is more. Words that at first sight seem simple enough often cause him real diffi-culties, because the surface meaning leaves room for different interpretations, which cannot at once, without further ado, be attributed to any definite objective dogmatic interest. And why should difference of opinion be confined to the explanation of Thucydides or Plato? Why should it not also occur in explaining the Bible, since the human authors, though God remains the principal agent, are fully active as instruments, in such a way that their writings are fully representative of their times?

The Inevitable Tension between Exegesis and Theology

The honest efforts of New Testament exegetes often fail fully to satisfy the 'outsiders'. In the course of their scientific efforts, conflicts, at least apparent ones, arise between the findings of exegetes and the subjects taught in systematic theology. The reason undoubtedly is in the peculiar stand-point of the Catholic exegete. As the Munich scholar, O. Kuss, emphasizes, he has two starting-points. One is of course the faith and teaching of the concrete Church of to-day. If that were his only starting-point, however, the expense of a special chair of New Testament exegesis could be spared the Church and State, and the subject could be left to other disciplines, especially to systematic and practical theology, which all draw on the New Testament as their primary source. But there is another, 'essential and fundamental' starting-point, the New Testament itself, 'as a document which is to be explained strictly according to the universally recognized methods of linguistic and historical research' (O. Kuss). So the Catholic exegete too must first of all ask what each writer certainly, probably or possibly meant to tell his actual readers; and the writers are many, speaking at different times, intent on making various points, using various sets of concepts.

The Catholic exegete must try to establish what particular situation each author had in mind, what questions, interests and objects he had in view, what dangers or deviations among his readers held his attention—what heresies, for instance. The exegete must remember that the New Testament books were originally written to be read separately, without reference to each other. They are not a continuous work in the literary sense, and above all, they do not claim to give an exhaustive account of the work of Jesus, as his revelation unfolded itself in work and word, nor of the life of the Church in the first century. All the writings of the New Testament, including the Gospels, are in themselves discontinuous and 'random' products, directed in a given situation, with a definite purpose, to a more or less clearly delimited group of readers. It was not without good reason that more than three hundred years passed before the formation of the New Testament canon was *de facto* completed, that is, till the twenty-seven books we know, and only these, were gathered by the Church authorities into a closed collection of sacred and inspired writings. The Church therefore could and did exist for nearly 400 years without possessing a 'Canon of the New Testament'.

The situation pointed to in our second section, on the world of the past, already presented us with many obscurities. But what is the consequence of the fact just mentioned, that the New Testament was the product of certain situations? We are thinking here less of the Gospels than of the other books of the New Testament. They give no immediate answer to all the questions which *might* arise from the problems which they pose, either directly or indirectly, or which were bound to arise in the course of time: and, as the history of the Church and of dogma shows, were answered, as indeed they had to be, if revelation was to remain valid and unaltered and be the efficacious power of God in every age. But, once more, it was not the New Testament itself which answered these questions directly. Problems which arose in the second century, but above all in the third and fourth, and were solved with the help of concepts from Greek philosophy, for instance the mystery of the person and nature of Jesus, need not have been posed, at least in these terms, by St Peter, St Paul and St John. Naturally the exegete will try to draw the connecting lines, as well as he can, between the New Testament and the later preaching of the faith in the Church. Or he will at least try to indicate the initial stages of the later development. But working as an exegete, he is far from having the answers to all the questions, even the vital ones, which later became urgent. Or his answers will lack the precision and confidence of a 'Denzinger', or of a catechism, or of modern manuals of dogmatic and moral theology.

When compared with later and present-day developments, therefore, the information offered by the exegete will, inevitably in many cases, seem to be full of tensions, 'wrong directions', and sometimes will even be wrongly regarded as including contradictions, and be too hastily pilloried as a sign of a lack of 'thinking with the Church', or at any rate of scientific incompetence. In reality, this state of affairs only confirms categorically, from the historical stand-point, the dogma which says that revelation is contained in 'written books and unwritten traditions' and thereby re-affirms the principle that there is such a thing as the *'propositio ecclesiae'*, a propounding of revelation by the Church, and a development in the consciousness of faith. In this connexion we may insist again that no book of the New Testament, nor even the New Testament as a whole, claims to present exhaustively the understanding of revelation which the Church had even in the first century, or the deductions it made implicitly or explicitly from what Christ had revealed. Above all, they do not pretend to draw all possible and necessary conclusions with regard to faith and morals, such as the future might bring. Only the existential exegesis of the life lived by the later Church could in reality do this (see K. Rahner, p. 35 above—though here one must ask if it is not asking too much of the Catholic New Testament scholar, if he must carry all the weight of historical proof for the theologian, in critical cases).

Many relevant examples could be given from all branches of dogmatic and moral theology, of which one is as follows. The New Testament attests in various ways, including the words of Jesus, the most important elements of the constitution and organization of the primitive Church. But in New Testament times, understandably from every point of view, the conditions did not exist for theological reflexion on the constitution and authority of the Church, nor for the formulation of the principle of the apostolic succession and the Primacy. The expectation of the Second Coming, the activity of the Apostles, the special role of the Spirit, did not allow for such reflexion, which the altered conditions of the following period naturally stimulated. 'The New Testament offers no systematic view on a closed revelation, closed even with regard to its consequences.' So O. Kuss is right in saying that the exegete, who tries to protect the text from all tendentious interpretations, 'by his very reserve, tries to safeguard the hitherto unexploited potentialities of the text which may still be concealed in it'.

The Distinctive Nature of New Testament Theology

From all that has been said, we can see the undeniable 'weakness' of any 'theology of the New Testament', which seeks to align theological statements drawn from individual items of exegesis, and present them in an organic connexion. Compared to later theology and its disciplined development and growth, the New Testament is still unreflective and not very explicit. The writers are agreed objectively on fundamentals, but it is impossible to reduce their assertions to the harmony of a system. They are distinguished, as those engaged in the pastoral ministry might do well to note, less by clear concepts and exact formulas than by the wealth of imagery, simile and parable in their language. Their world of concepts, compared to that of later times, is often fluid, blurred, haphazard and uncritical—like the way people think—and at time is remarkably careless. The main reason is that many questions which were important later were simply not yet thought of, through no fault of the exegete, and misleading deductions were not yet to be feared.

However, even in the New Testament we can notice that some progress is being made from an unreflective mode of expression to a more self-conscious one. For instance, in the Gospel of St Mark, we read of strong emotions being displayed by Jesus. The Gospels of St Matthew and St Luke, which made use of St Mark's, have either softened the expressions or eliminated them. Again, Mark 3:21 says that 'the relatives of Jesus wished to overpower him, for, they said, he is out of his mind'. St Matthew and St Luke, when working over this section, omit the episode entirely. They do so independently of each other, as is usually acknowledged, and almost certainly to prevent the readers drawing unfortunate conclusions.

In spite of all this, the advantages of a theology of the New Testament must not be overlooked. It is, of its very nature, something more than theorizing and systematizing, since it is nothing else than the Gospel, the proclamation of the 'wonderful works of God', the attestation of an undreamt-of experience and possibility. It is an address to the readers which wishes to stir their hearts. It is the preaching, the experience of a great newness that still rings resoundingly from its pages; the conscious testimony to something directly experienced, the sense of being gripped by the event of Christ and the mystery of Christ, joy at the onset of the hour of salvation, at belonging to the new people of God, which is the inheritor of salvation, the living exciting hope of the coming fulfilment of redemption. All this could again be illustrated by striking examples.

The Elaboration of New Methods and the Broadening Basis of Research

Why does research now pose problems and give answers which since the war are audible in Catholic circles, but which thirty years ago or more, were scarcely voiced? The reason is mainly the development and verification of new methods of scientific research. The older methods, concerned with the history of ideas and of religions, grew in importance as instructive material was constantly added to the sources available. Among these methods were also criticism of sources and literary analysis. These latter received an objectively necessary extension by means of two new methods, which were applied above all to Gospel research. The first was the method of form-criticism (*Form-geschichte*), which came in after the first world war and which can also be called by the more general name of 'the method of the history of traditions'. It tries to go behind the oldest attainable written sources in Gospel research, to reach the pre-literary stages of the tradition about Jesus. It tries to place each element of tradition in its setting in the life of Jesus and of the Easter Church, striving to show how the traditional matter was moulded in course of transmission. The second, to complete the first, came after the second world war and can be called the method of 'history of redaction'. This investigates the special ways in which the raw material offered by tradition was worked over by each of the evangelists, with their differing theological attitudes and aims.

Form-criticism in particular started to investigate the Gospels from what were often very radically sceptical pre-suppositions about the contents of the Gospels. Hence it often reached untenable results. But when used properly it led to a closer acquaintance with the tradition and doctrine embodied in the New Testament, and gave new insight into the literary and theological distinctiveness of each book. This was particularly true of the Gospels, which like all the books of the New Testament, were composed to be put at the service of the preachers. All the New Testament books proclaim the message of salvation, the Gospels differently from the other books, and the Gospel of St John again differently from the first three (Synoptic) Gospels, the real letters differently from the epistles, the book of the Apocalypse differently from the Acts of the Apostles.

All that was needed on the Catholic side was a directive from the teaching authority of the Church. This came when the encyclical of Pius XII on 'the proper promotion of biblical studies to-day' opened up the way on September 30, 1943. It allowed and commended the proper adaptation of all well-tried methods of scientific research to the whole Bible. Accordingly, in Germany after the war, a perceptible thrust forward was made in lecture-halls and publications, a movement which had been prepared in the dens of scholars during the time of silence imposed by Nazism and the second world war. And one may say without exaggeration that New Testament research has during this same period gained a hearing and an esteem even among 'laymen', such as one would hardly have dared to dream of a few decades ago.

The Shock of 'Novelties'

The impression of the layman that New Testament studies have awakened to completely new methods and analyses is perfectly correct. But there it is! Progress in any discipline always has emotional repercussions. I myself am also shocked when, for instance, I hear to-day from theologians certain explanations which as a student I neither heard of, nor read in the good old manuals. Probably my shock is due to the fact that I am too little abreast of theology. So too with the 'outsider' when he hears of to-day's exegesis, with its hypotheses and questions. He hears that the Synoptics and St John are very different types of gospels, that even the Synoptics diverge strongly from one another, and thus that they give rise to the question of the changes undergone by the tradition about Jesus, of the original form of his sayings, and of the contribution of the primitive preaching as it transmitted these words and the history of Jesus and applied them to the situation created by

Easter. And then when he hears of a concrete example, such as Matthew 28:19 of which we spoke above, he feels extremely hesitant, suspicious and even indignant. And it may happen that before he has had time to orientate himself even crudely with regard to the facts, much less test the case by means of a set of 'Gospel Parallels' or, say, a new edition of Schmid's commentaries, he pounces on a satisfactory explanation of these scandalous novelties: 'The New Testament scholars of to-day are again more or less parroting the Protestants!'

No one can have more sympathy for this feeling of shock than one of ourselves, who have taken years of concentrated study to form gradually an independent judgment, going through in the process a metamorphosis which was more painful than refreshing. But we have also learnt that the matter is not to be dismissed so lightly. And I think that we should speak our minds honestly about such slogans as the above, which is not entirely without foundation when to-day an exegete of great distinction and an authoritative theologian like Cardinal Bea is head of the Secretariat for the Promoting of Christian Unity in the Council. An exegesis or hypothesis which was perhaps first put forward by Protestants has not the advantage of greater objectivity as a matter of course. The Protestant scholar comes to the New Testament with prejudices, at least as regards his profession of faith and therefore of a dogmatic nature, just as much as the Catholic. Often enough he is far more influenced from the start by an *a priori* presupposition which determines his attitudes and his philosophy. The best example of this is the strong trend towards the existentialist interpretation of the message of Jesus and the primitive Church, an interpretation which is the decisive factor in all discussions among Protestants, and is often at work even when such expressions as 'de-mythizing' and 'existentialist' are avoided to spare shocking the orthodox.

No one will say, however, that an exegesis or a hypothesis which has been worked out scientifically must be heretical or at least false merely because it was first propounded by an Evangelical theologian. After all, the New Testament itself is not a heretical book! And it can hardly be denied that in the field of New Testament studies we have gained from the Protestant side not merely the impulse towards new methods but also basic attitudes and insights, guiding lines which Catholic scholars could not but follow in the long run. There are of course good reasons for this. They are not to our discredit just because they are due to certain structures. Because of their principle of the 'Bible alone', Protestants have taken a wider and more intensive interest in scientific work on the New Testament. Further, and in consequence of this, the number of chairs at the universities and of fully-formed experts has been incomparably greater among the Protestants. And they were not bound by any teaching authority in the Catholic sense.

In practice, the Catholic scholar is inclined to be timorous. In spite of the express statement of the encyclical *Divino Afflante Spiritu* in this regard, he shrinks from being the first in the field with a new hypothesis, lest it bring him under suspicion, even when it does not affect dogma or at least does not contradict it, but just because it is new. Protestant authors are free of such inhibitions. They develop and test new methods, they try one hypothesis after another without any embarrassment. Much of their product may prove to be chaff, or more or less artificial reconstruction, or at any rate the one-sided exaggeration of a correct view-point. But within this gay multiplication of hypotheses, one finds all the same a large number of fruitful individual observations, a series of hypotheses worthy of serious discussion, and finally a percentage which under the microscope of mutual criticism hold their ground as new acquisitions. Without wanting to, the Catholic exegete is often forced, on his own presuppositions, to test critically for method and contents the result of Protestant discussion, which has nearly always been in the vanguard. He has to make his own what has been tested and found true, and to develop it as best he can. Many Catholics, in anything but official ecclesiastical positions, seem to think that as long as a conservative position, for instance about the authorship of a book, is maintained by any Protestant scholars—fundamentalists or pietists perhaps—it should still be upheld by Catholics. Some might like to force such a principle of external authority on the Catholic scholar, instead of keeping to the basic rule of 'a position is as good as its proofs'. They would thereby make it quite impossible for him to take an independent lead. At any rate, if the Catholic scholar has to work to a great extent in constant exchange of criticism with Evangelical scholarship, and finds there convincing items of knowledge, that is of itself no ground for suspicion.

Church authority itself provides a confirmation of this. We take as an instance the case in which an official organ of the Church, the Biblical Commission, committed itself to a disciplinary decision in the interests of truth to be discovered. At the beginning of the century the famous 'Two-Sources' theory had been worked out in essentials. Somewhat later came the decisions of the Biblical Commission on the Synoptic Gospels. The decisions had good results. The above-mentioned explanation of the literary relationships of the three oldest gospels was tested critically from all angles. Other hypotheses to solve the Synoptic problem were tried. Finally the Two-Sources theory was recognized in principle as for the time being at least the most solid, straight-forward and really practicable hypothesis. Since then Catholic publications, including those of the Pontifical Biblical Institute, take the kernel of the theory for granted without misgivings. They hold the priority of St Mark's Gospel, and explain the traditional material, which St Matthew and St. Luke have in common beyond St Mark, as coming from a collection of matter used by both St Matthew and St Luke.

Magistra or Ancilla Theologiae?

Finally, there is no serious danger that New Testament science and theology will shoot up too high and proud among its fellow-disciplines. Outwardly, it stands too much in the most advanced front of theological discussion at present for that, and being notoriously engaged on research into foundations, it has to bear the main brunt of disputation. It has to face the concrete texts and their problems, where other disciplines can ignore the individual texts or leave their value as proofs undecided, without being untrue to their proper tasks. Inside, within the organism of Catholic theology, it of course keeps necessarily its magisterial function, in so far as it is, to the extent above indicated, the sounding-board of the voice of Jesus and the Church of his Apostles, which is the *norma non normanda* of the knowledge of the faith. But even to-day it wishes, in accordance with the depths of its being, to be nothing else than it always was, the *ancilla theologiae*, the handmaid of theology, serving systematic and especially dogmatic theology with all its might.

To-day's New Testament scholar must understand this ancillary function better than ever, and feel it more profoundly than ever. As never before, the research of the last decades has made him aware that the New Testament is no independent and self-subsistent entity which came into existence more or less before the Church and outside the Church, and is thus to some extent a self-sufficient and responsible authority which could be opposed to the Church, which came to life since Pentecost. Not only the Canon of the New Testament, but also all the books of what was later called the New Testament—including the Gospels, the most extensive accounts we have of the 'historical' Jesus, the founder of Christianity—were written in the service of the preaching of the Church, and went forth from her bosom. They are entirely a function of the Church which taught and sent out missionaries, which gave exhortations and decisions, which lived and acted sacramentally, and was in existence for years and tens of years before the Gospels were written. It is for these reasons that the Church, rightly even from the purely historical point of view, proclaims herself the ultimate competent and authentic interpreter of these, *her* sacred books.

Heinrich
Schlier

THE MEANING AND FUNCTION
OF A THEOLOGY OF
THE NEW TESTAMENT

The notion of what a theology of the New Testament, or a biblical theology, should be has often changed in the two hundred years of its history. Even to-day there is no general agreement, though the field is being intensively cultivated, as is shown by the appearance of a number of works covering the whole subject and countless monographies on particular items. The considerations which follow can only be a supplement to the discussion which is already taking place, a contribution from an author— and this is their advantage and disadvantage—to whom the question itself is still open.

The name of our field of work has indeed hardly changed at all, and to-day it is by general consent the title for very different types of books. This shows that the name has obviously anticipated for a long time the nature of the undertaking. Thus the title can be a sort of guiding star for our enquiry, the means of clarifying the principles and of grasping the meaning and task of a general presentation of New Testament theology.

As the name implies, indicating the subject beforehand, this is a theology of the *New* Testament. This brings in elements which should tell in its general presentation. At the very least it means that our work deals with the concepts, expressed or implied, of the New Testament and with no others. It is based exclusively on texts taken from the New Testament. They are put before the biblical theologian by the Church as part of the inspired and sacred Scriptures. They dominate, at various levels, in her preaching, her catechism, her liturgy. Dogmatic theology is constantly preoccupied with them because they are the primary source of its information. Exegesis strives to disclose the meaning of each particular text, and the 'Introduction to the New Testament' tries to throw light on their history and literary forms, by tracing the course of the earliest transmission of the texts. Since it is the theology of Scripture which presents itself in such an ecclesiastical and theological context, its procedures, its set of concepts, its methods, its themes and even the basic structure of its presentation must be derived from its object and from nowhere else.

This means first of all that a New Testament theology questions the various books, or groups of writings, of which the New Testament consists, as to their theology. For the New Testament is composed of writings whose origin, contents, forms, intentions and meaning are very different, as exegesis and 'Introduction' show. The nature of the matters treated make it therefore preferable to begin, when seeking the basic theological principles of the New Testament, by investigating it in the light of the manifold diversity of the books. This naturally demands the procedure which has been elaborated in exegesis, and in general in the explanation of historical texts. This is the philological and historical method, which has as its object the straight-forward delineation and description of the theological contents of each particular book. To live up to its name, a theology of the New Testament must allow its concepts to be formed for it by the New Testament. This will always be a matter of approximation, for its world of concepts can only impose itself on the interpreter in so far as they silence his own, once the contents are really grasped. But on principle, a theology of the New Testament must tend towards a set of concepts suited to it, which are not scholastic or idealist, nor those of modern philosophy. They are pre-philosophical and pre-theological, and yet not just naïve. Their simplicity is radical, and couched in a language which is often polished. Literal translation will not do the job, and the speech of biblical theology cannot be just the 'language of Canaan' or popular piety, as is clear. This would merely show that the intention of the New Testament has not been grasped.

Further, theology of the New Testament means that the themes must be presented by the New Testament itself, with all the variety and all the limitations which appear there. No doubt all the basic themes of theology are touched on somehow or other, and many are developed in different sets of variations. Thus for instance Christology, ecclesiology and eschatology come to mind. Other themes appear only marginally, as for instance creation; and for others only the key-word is given, as for instance in the weighty theme of offices in the Church. All this must be taken into consideration in a theology of the New Testament. At any rate, its subjects will not be imposed on it by a mature, that is, a highly developed dogmatic theology.

Finally, a theology of the New Testament will prove

itself to be such by handling the themes set it by the
New Testament in the way indicated to it in each
case by the various books of the New Testament. It
will pay attention to the basic movement of thought
in each book or group of books, and try to integrate
their intention into the structure of its presentation.
Thus, to my mind, the theology of the New Testament,
when dealing with St Paul, will develop his theology as a
function of the Event, in whose basic traits he sees comprehended the history and existence of mankind. This is
the resurrection of Jesus Christ, the crucified Lord, who
has been exalted in view of his Coming, so that his being
raised up was an eschatological or final act.

If one tries to meet all these demands, which the New
Testament itself—as exegesis, form-criticism and history
of tradition have taught us to understand it—imposes on
its theology, the theology of the New Testament presents
at first a very remarkable picture. It is composed of a whole
series of theologies, each with very different horizons,
stand-points and ways of looking at things, with concepts
developed in very different ways and often diverging in
content, with themes of many kinds, or simply hints of
themes, and with basic structures which vary widely. On
the whole, it is a theology, or rather a collection of different theologies, of a markedly fragmentary character. Often
the lines are not fully drawn. A theological statement is
intoned, it rings out here and there, and then suddenly
is buried again in deep silence. A presentation of New
Testament theology will have to pay particular attention
to this, even though in consequence subjects may appear to
be treated with little regard to their true proportions.
However, this character of the fragmentary is shared by
New Testament theology, as a matter of principle, with

dogmatic or speculative theology. This latter is indeed systematic, but this does not mean that it could, somewhat like a system of philosophy, offer a system that would be in any way comprehensive and complete. In this sense the words of 1 Corinthians 13:9, 'We know . . . in part', hold good for dogmatic theology too.

But let us now look at the other element. A New Testament theology is by virtue of name and concept also a *theology* of the New Testament. That means firstly, as regards tendencies that are still at work to-day, a very formal contrast. New Testament theology does not set out to be the presentation of a historical process. It is not at all a history of the religion of primitive Christianity. Nor is it a history of New Testament theology. From the stand-point of a history of primitive Christianity, and indeed from a purely 'historical' stand-point in general, a theology of the New Testament is an absurdity, first of all because it is 'theology' and then because historically there is no justification for restricting it to the collection of books in the New Testament. Such a restriction is already a piece of theology, and the starting-point of New Testament theology. E. Stauffer indeed maintains that this is what entitles it to the name of theology. But this is a mistake. He has indeed taken the title 'theology' seriously, because in his 'Theology of the New Testament' he does not describe a process immanent to history, the 'development' of a religion. He tries to give the transcendent process of salvation and its Christocentric history. But history, even the theology of history, is not enough to make up a theol-ogy, not even the theology of the New Testament. It fails most completely when this 'theology of history'—as the benevolent critic J. Jeremias remarked about Stauffer—is in danger of becoming a 'Gnosis of the process of salvation'.

However, the name 'theology of the New Testament' of course means more than a formal contrast to any sort of presentation of history, important though this demarcation may be. As we have seen, when the New Testament is interrogated for its theology it answers first of all by giving various theologies, according to each group of writings and, indeed, according to individual books. There is for instance a distinctive theology of the Epistle to the Hebrews. But the name of our discipline, and therefore the concept foreshadowed by it, is not concerned merely with a number of different theologies. It has *one* in view, *the* theology of the New Testament. This it claims to produce because there exists a previous theological conviction of the unity of the New Testament, which has in the course of a long process impressed itself on the mind of the Church and received its approbation.

The claim to unity is also based on the concept and essence of theology. It is true that theology, meaning primarily dogmatic theology, is never more than a fragmentary presentation. But just as surely, it presupposes a hidden, inner unity which is always present. This is precisely what is indicated by its systematic character. The end and object is to draw the hidden unity out of its concealment as much as possible, and to make it known. And only so far as it is *en route*, so to speak, to this inner unity, do its particular propositions show themselves in their full light. For the place they have in this inner unity is given them by God. The same holds good for a theology of the New Testament. Hence its presentation must always look to the inner unity and take the way to this goal. The task must not be performed too hastily; the immediate discrepancies in theological views must not be overlooked or passed by. But the more the presentation penetrates into the central unity of the theology of the New Testament, the more it will be theology.

How is it possible to penetrate through all its variety to the unity of the theology of the New Testament? At this point New Testament theology shows clearly that it needs not only the methods of history and philology, but also a method of theology. Such a method is of course always needed, but here the question as to its nature becomes more acute. Indeed, it would perhaps be better not to say 'method', and rather ask: by what route shall we gain entrance to the real content; on what road does the reality spoken of by the New Testament disclose itself? The way is open to one only in so far as one actually marches along it. And by this we mean that while one must make full use of historical criticism and linguistic research, one must also be involved in the reality which confronts one in the texts of the New Testament. But this involvement takes place in the act of faith!

In any case, the historical and philological approach is never enough to disclose the sense of a historical text. To confine oneself to history and linguistics when reading Plato, without ever giving oneself over to his thought, which means—since his thought is no isolated process— without ever trying to share his experience, would be to miss for ever the vision of reality which Plato discovered and from which he lived and thought. Something of the same kind is true of all historical texts. Interpretation, when it really reaches the heart of the matter, is never just a technique: it is a vital process. One could apply all the instruments available from history and linguistics to inter- preting the New Testament, but never yield oneself to the basic experience out of which the New Testament itself speaks, that is, faith. If so, one would never recognize the reality which finds utterance in the New Testament.

In saying this, we do not mean to disregard the demand which the New Testament, as a document from ancient times, makes upon us, namely that we translate it objectively, using the means offered by historical science and philology. And likewise, we do not thereby mean to turn the faith into a method. But we mean that the interpretation of the New Testament is also to become part of our own real experience, as should all interpretation. The historical and linguistic explanation of the New Testament must be at the service of faith, if it is to reach through the text to the thing itself and the intrinsic connexions of things. Here this means to have insight into the links of salvation, as described in the theology of the New Testament.

The theology of the New Testament, like every theology which presents the faith, is a matter of the *intellectus fidei*. As C. Spicq says: 'The object of this theology is not the words nor even the thoughts of the inspired writers, but the reality itself to which they bear witness. The theologian, convinced of the objectivity of revelation and of its radical unity, scrutinizes the divine mystery in its biblical expression. He discerns for example all the components of a certain theme, gives precisions about their articulation and development, allots full value to its multiple aspects, displays its connexions with other themes, and using its enunciations but reaching beyond them, gives the believer the possibility of attaining the divine object itself' (*Revue Biblique*, 1951). The *intellectus fidei*, therefore, penetrates to the thing itself (*res*), and its unity, and so constitutes itself as theology. Thereby the theology of the New Testament proves itself to be an involvement of the person in history, not just a historical science.

This means here that it is a science where the personal history of him who practises it is involved, a science in whose exercise the practitioner must let his own history, his 'existence', be determined and moulded by that which is disclosed in the course of interpretation. One cannot practise a science which has to do with history, unless one surrenders one's own personal history to the word which confronts him, from the pages of a history which at first was external to him. Faith is the necessary self-surrender to the history which addresses us from the New Testament. In faith I tread the path upon which the Church, always going before me, has met this history, in order to meet it ever anew. The theology of the New Testament presses on to the reality of the matter, there thought of and expressed, reaches its unity and so raises itself to be a theology, if and in so far as it is itself a personally historical process, none other than the movement of the *intellectus fidei*, the thinking of the faith.

From this way of understanding New Testament theology, there now follow certain consequences for its structure. Where is this theology to make a start if it is to realize its concept? M. Meinertz (*Theologie des Neuen Testaments,* 1950) says that 'by the nature of things', the presentation of Jesus and his doctrine must come at the beginning of New Testament theology. Hence the first major section of his book deals with the teaching person and history of Jesus. R. Bultmann (*Theologie des Neuen Testaments,*[2] 1954) says that New Testament theology begins only with the Kerygma, the preaching of the primitive community, so that Jesus' own proclamation cannot be part of a theology of the New Testament, though as a presupposition it must be allowed its say. So he puts it as the first section of the first part of his 'Theology', where he develops the 'Presuppositions and Themes of New Testament Theology'. The second section deals with the 'Preaching of the Primitive Community', a third with the 'Preaching of the Hellenistic Community Before and After Paul'. But is this not to let historical view-points dominate theology; or, as the case may be, is this not to introduce the *genre* of history into theology? What has a history or a 'picture' of Jesus to do with the presentation of the theology of the New Testament? Jesus, after all, did not begin the theology of the New Testament; and the theological reflexions of the New Testament writers are not continuations of the theological reflexions of Jesus. Of course, the Event of Jesus, his person, actions and words, preceded the theology of the New Testament writers, so that there is no such thing as New Testament theology apart from this Event. But in what way did it precede the theology of the New Testament?

Briefly, in this way: the history of Jesus, which called forth faith, makes the theological enunciations of the New Testament possible, being their *raison d'être* in every way. It is 'the Call, the answer to which is first represented by the testimony to faith, given by the primitive community'. Thus far J. Jeremias, from whom this formulation is taken, and Bultmann, who means the same thing, are correct. But Jeremias apparently means by the Call only the preaching of Jesus. And Stauffer is therefore correct in countering him—and thereby Bultmann—by saying: 'To the self-revelation of Jesus belong not only his word but his actions, his life and his death'. Since the whole history of Jesus is involved, Stauffer says that he sees no possibility of 'presenting Jesus Christ, really and fully, within the framework of a biblical theology' (*Evangelische Luth. Kirchenzeitung*, 1950).

But is there not also a reason why on principle we should not insert the history of Jesus into the presentation of the theology of the New Testament, not even as its presupposition? Have we any access at all to Jesus and to his history, except by means of the 'personal-historical' approach, that is, by means of an interpretation of the gospels which is given by faith, and therefore through the witnesses who are the authoritative interpreters of the life of Jesus, and who alone can reveal it? We ask this question not merely on the practical grounds that form-criticism and history of tradition have shown how inextricably narrative and interpretation, story and message, are interwoven. The historical interpretation which prescinds from the interpretation and the message of the Evangelists leaves scarcely anything over!

However this negative result, which comes from very careful investigations of acknowledged worth, is only a symptom of the reason given by the nature of the matter itself, that is, by the person and the history of Jesus. We put the question therefore also on theological grounds. Is the Jesus of whom the gospels speak, is the 'real' Jesus, the Jesus Christ of this earth in his history, accessible to us in any other way, except as he was known and attested by the witnesses in the light of the faith of Easter? Is the real Jesus ever disclosed to us, except in the interpretation of the witnesses, who objectively refuse to disregard faith as the presupposition of their knowledge? Has the real Jesus ever been anyone but he who was so known and attested? Is there an 'historical' Jesus, to be grasped by 'historical' means? Is not the so-called 'historical' Jesus

7

either the real challenging (*geschichtlich*) Jesus of the gospels—or one disclosed in a fundamentally inappropriate way, namely, apart from the *intellectus fidei*? Such a Jesus would not be truly disclosed but only invented, thought out that is, by historical fantasy. Here then is the theological reason for our question, a reason however which is precisely proved true by historical research. Is there a Jesus except as he comes by the word of the Church, from the very beginning and by the nature of things?

The meagre success of every effort at arriving at a 'life of Jesus', their heavy-handed psychology and fantasy confirm the fact that from the very start and by his nature Jesus only exists for us through and throughout the gospels, that is, in the voice of the Church, which alone renders his reality as it is. However, we must go back a little. The history of Jesus is the presupposition, not a part of New Testament theology. Here we mean his whole history, the event of his person, his deeds and his word. The whole event however reaches us in its full and undisguised reality only in the answer which the gospels, and indeed the whole testimony of the New Testament give. The gospels, which embraced and expounded that history (rhema: 'word') in their 'word' (rhema) must be the first to be interrogated as to their exposition, so that their theology may be quarried out.

It is significant therefore that Stauffer, Meinertz and Bultmann, each for different reasons, omit all systematic treatment of the theology of the Synoptic Gospels. As we have already pointed out (see p. 95 f), Bultmann's outline in the first part of his work confines itself to history, as even the titles of the sections show. It is the same in the third part of the work, which bears the very revealing title: 'The Developement from Which the Ancient Church

Arose'. Here the discussion ranges for the most part outside the New Testament writings. Only the second part of his work has as headings, 'The Theology of Paul', 'The Theology of John'. And this is the only part where theological content dominates the arrangement. Thus the very outline of the whole work makes it clear that, according to Bultmann, only St Paul and St John have theologies in the proper sense of the word.

Admittedly, there is a question here. Can a New Testament theology begin with a presentation of that of the Synoptics, without more ado? Chronologically—though that does not matter—and even causally, was it not preceded by another theology, because the Synoptic testimony was preceded by another? When one interrogates the New Testament, do there not exist before all its books and all its theology, certain concrete testimonies, which already contain theological enunciations, and indeed precisely those which were to dominate the whole theology of the New Testament as it took shape in the books? Even before there were any New Testament writings, had not the 'word' of the history of Jesus Christ crystallized into formulations and did these not impose themselves in various ways on the New Testament writings, in the form of the confession of faith of the primitive Church? These formulas are the primary utterance of the revelation of Jesus Christ as it voiced itself. They are the primary response of the Community as it threw itself open to him. Do they not therefore carry within them the primary explanation of the salvific act of God in Jesus Christ, an explicitation which is then developed in the New Testament writings and their proclamation and their theology? (See the author's *Die Zeit der Kirche*, 1956. R. Schnackenburg speaks of the 'primitive apostolic preaching of salvation' and the 'community theology based upon it' as the 'first steps of primitive Christian theology'.)

In fact, the history of New Testament tradition has shown us with ever-increasing clarity that the New Testament writings enshrine a number of fixed traditions of the faith, and in particular formulas of the faith, which give a stamp to the books and to their proclamation, consciously or unconsciously. A fixed form of transmission, for instance, decisively influenced the formation of the Passion narrative and the theology behind it. Outlines of the original proclamation of the faith and certain formulas of belief come up constantly and at decisive moments in the Acts of the Apostles and the New Testament epistles, and then make themselves felt as the rule of faith developed in the texts. Thus, to take one example which may stand for others, the normative 'good word' which St Paul cites in 1 Corinthians 15 : 3–5, is used by the Apostle himself as the basis of his theological explanation of the resurrection of the dead in 1 Corinthians 15. In the Epistle to the Hebrews, a confession of faith is expounded by texts of Scripture used in an esoteric way (*Schriftgnosis*). Must not a theology of the New Testament take this fact into account and therefore try first of all to present the archaic theology of these authoritative primary forms of the Message, the theology which is unfolded in the writings of the New Testament?

This is of course a very difficult undertaking. For it includes working out on different levels those traditions and formulas of the faith which were minted in the primitive Church, and which then continued to colour the expositions which followed. This study would leave many questions open simply on account of the state of our sources, but it is above all the extremely fragmentary character of the relatively few recognizable primitive formulas of revelation which makes it hard to grasp the theological thoughts which find expression in them. All the same one will be able to ascertain certain theological principles which form the effective basis of the theology of the New Testament writings, a theology which is both bound by them and develops them. This makes it clear that the theology which expresses itself in the New Testament writings already implies the presence before its eyes of the apostolic tradition, as the proximate source of faith. To expound the theology of this proximate source of faith for New Testament theology would not be to import a foreign body.

With this as a starting-point, the theology of the New Testament writings could then be presented as the exposition of these basic traditions. And here the sequence of the writings and groups of writings to be interrogated for their theology will play a role. This sequence is hard to fix clearly. But at any rate, the date of origin of this book or that cannot be accepted as the decisive word. Nor will one be able simply to follow the order of the books in the Canon, for this order had other than theological causes. Undoubtedly, the Acts of the Apostles will be investigated along with the Gospel of St Luke, and the Epistles of St John along with his gospel. To organize the work, one could perhaps take the proximity of content in a given book or group of books, with regard to the underlying formulated traditions of faith, and likewise the degree of development in the theology in question.

At any rate, one will first treat the theology of each of the Synoptic Gospels. For these are, if one may say so, none other than an interpretation and expansion, from their several proper theological stand-points, of a common tradition of faith and preaching, somewhat in the form which Acts 10:36–43 still preserves for us. In all the Synoptic Gospels the Lord Jesus Christ is meant to speak, he whose death and resurrection (and manifest Coming) were a certain truth of faith, and who spoke in his whole historical coming—in his word and in his deeds, which were already gathered and circulated orally, and to some extent in writing. The theology of these gospels may be deciphered above all from the manner in which they interpreted, arranged and modified each item of the contents of tradition. (See W. Hillmann in *Wissenschaft und Weisheit*, 1951; R. Schnackenburg, above, p. 114.) The 'studies in the theology of St Luke' by H. Conzelmann are exemplary from the point of view of method in such work. But even his work shows how much a theology of the New Testament has still to accomplish at this point. The theology of St Luke could of course only be derived from the whole gospel, including therefore chapters 1 and 2, and from the Acts of the Apostles. Part of the theology is precisely the fact that the Evangelist St Luke takes the salvific history of the Lord Jesus Christ back even to his birth, and continues it in the history of his 'Name', which is also the history of the Holy Spirit in the Apostles and in the Church till its constitution in Rome.

It is hard to decide whether the theology of the individual Synoptics, including the Acts of the Apostles, should be followed by the theology of the Pauline or of the Johannine writings. For taking the latter first, we have grounds in the fact that it too seems to offer a theological interpretation of the basic preaching, in the form of a gospel. But if one looks closer, one recognizes how far the Gospel of St John has departed from the synoptic concept of how a basic outline of the preaching may be expanded and filled out from historical material still available. The fourth gospel is very deliberately an interpretation of the well-worked-out gospel matter which lay before him, very like that of our Synoptics, but not identical with it. And the interpretation which follows is given from the stand-point which was already authoritative, but which is now made express and thought out in its consequences: that the history of Jesus is the history of the Word, and must also be presented as such. The Logos (Word) in its action, and the action of the Word, must be presented in a gospel. This the Gospel of St John shows clearly on every page, so that it is monstrous, for instance, to separate the so-called prologue from the rest of the gospel when handling the theology of this gospel.

But the theological reflexion of this gospel is also strongly developed in other respects. This can be seen for instance in its doctrine of the Spirit, and above all from something that is mostly under the surface but is very active, namely its reflexion on the sacraments and on the Church. Finally, the Johannine theology, if we take in also the Johannine epistles, already casts its net very wide. The salvific action of the Word is expressly and frequently considered in its effects on the existence of man, whom the Word has assumed. And if the Apocalypse, which at any rate shows objective points of contact with the Gospel of St John, is to be dealt with here also—and I do not know where else it can be placed—then the scope of Johannine theology becomes even greater. For the so-called revelation of St John continues, if one looks at it from a theological stand-point, the history of the Word made flesh, in so far as it uncovers the process of his Coming in the fate of the world, through and throughout its history, and thereby shows itself to be a prophetic gospel.

With these peculiar properties of the Johannine writings in mind, one will rather develop the Pauline theology in the second section, in a theology of the New Testament. The Apostle St Paul writes no gospel. But from a theological point of view, he is closer to the Synoptic Gospels than the Gospel of St John. His epistles let us see how closely he in particular links up with the formulas of faith of the primitive Church and its other traditions. The basic experience which he had on the road to Damascus provided for him personally the certainty of the legitimacy of his gospel and his apostolate. Theologically it marked out for him his horizon, and determined his outlook. Still, it is not for him the source and object of his theology. What he thinks over theologically, in the certainty and illumination communicated to him at Damascus and by the light there received, are the traditions of faith handed on by the primitive community, in which traditions the Lord speaks for St Paul. (This remains true, even if one does not accept entirely the explanation of 1 Corinthians 11:23 put forward by O. Cullmann.)

St Paul links up with the traditions by a manifold interpretation of the Christological message, and in manifold ponderings of its consequences for the existence of man and the history of the world. And this link-up, as it does its work of interpretation and develops its consequences, is accomplished often by him in conscious theological argumentation and in relatively developed theological concepts. All this is precisely the reason why the Pauline theology is the easiest to grasp, and occupies spontaneously the major portion of a theology of the New Testament. The Epistles of St Paul, the legacy which has been preserved to us in writing, are also the only writings of the New Testament which allow us to place this or that item of theology in something like a line of development; or better, which allows us to see traces of different levels of theological thinking.

The Pauline theology, on account of its close links with the tradition of the community which, to be sure, it unfolds on the basis of a personal experience and in a theology developed independently, may then be placed before the Johannine. And if this be accepted, one will continue it with the theology of the other New Testament epistles which remain. Here of course the first epistle of St Peter and the Epistle to the Hebrews are the most weighty. The theology which is at work in them and which they put forward also rests on acquired and developed traditions of faith. The smaller epistles of the New Testament have likewise their own place within the totality of New Testament theology. But this still does not mean that they offer even remotely a complete theology, so that for instance one would be entitled to speak of a 'concept of doctrine' in the Epistle of St Jude. Investigating these epistles for theological propositions will heighten our awareness that New Testament theology is composed primarily of a number of fragments of theology.

To be sure, with this presentation of the theological structure of the individual books or groups of writings in the New Testament, the task of writing a theology of the New Testament has not been performed. And if what has been said above about the nature and exigencies of a 'theology' is to be observed carefully even in the investigation of the theology of individual books and groups of writings, it is all the more important when we come to the point where we must leave individual items and come to the theology of the whole, of the New Testament. The task of composing such a theology is only done when we have succeeded in showing the unity of the different 'theologies'. Only then does the name make sense and the concept of 'a theology' find verification. That there is such a unity, that ultimately there is no contradiction between the various theological principles and utterances, is from the point of view of theology a presupposition which derives from the inspiration and canonicity of the New Testament or the Bible. The unity thus envisaged is however a real one, not one so mysteriously hidden that it cannot be made known at least at a certain level. The structure of this unity may already be glimpsed in the elementary theology of those formulas of faith which have influenced to a greater or lesser extent the whole of the New Testament. And now, when the theology of the individual sources has been brought to light, its unity must be made as explicit as possible.

How is this to be done? The best way, no doubt, is to take some major themes, such as God, the Reign of God, Jesus Christ, his death and resurrection, the Spirit, the Church, the new life, the faith and so on, and use them to indicate how the various theologies are intrinsically re-lated to each other. In this way the hidden basis and the mysterious bond of the single New Testament theology will be illuminated. This is a difficult undertaking, and one which must skirt many dangers. One such danger is that the individuality of the theological conception of a given book may lose again the contours which have been drawn for it, when the unity of New Testament theology is put too much into the foreground. For this unity is a background. Another danger is that we might—expressly or otherwise—make the theology of one book or group of books the norm of what is 'Theology of the New Testament' and try to arrange all other theological concepts to fit it.

The theology of the New Testament is built on the basis of all the New Testament writings, though of course not all of them contribute in the same proportion.

One must also avoid the temptation of trying to find the unity of New Testament theology merely in the unity of a single basic theme, as for instance in the so-called 'Event of Christ'. Here misgivings should arise, not only because the theology of the New Testament would thus be reduced to Christology, but because the real task would be lost sight of, which is precisely to show the unity of the different interpretations of the 'Even⸱ of Christ'. Finally, one will try to avoid leaving the unity of New Testament theology too much to generalities. Like every real theology, it must be concrete to be authentic.

Here I might add my own opinion that one must not let it all come down to the developed credal formulas of the ancient Church, as though the Creeds were the result of New Testament theology and the title-deeds of its unity. These formulas have been discussed very helpfully by Stauffer and Meinertz. But we must remember that the primitive formulas of faith were at hand in the Church even before the New Testament, and that the ancient Creeds do not derive solely from the New Testament. The historical process was more or less that both oral and written traditions came together and were crystallized in the Creeds, and that the apostolic heritage was committed independently in each case to Scripture and to the Creeds. The processes influenced each other reciprocally.

For an integral theology of the New Testament one more thing is wanted. We must demonstrate its basic unity with that of the Old Testament, or show its relation to Old Testament theology. After all, it is only in combination with the Old Testament that the New has the character of Sacred and Canonical Scripture. As things are to-day, however, it will be a long time before such a condition is more than a wish. For here too over-hasty and patchwork solutions will not do. And why should not a theological science confess its limitations and its deficiencies in a given epoch? It must only keep in mind, recalling it constantly by means of individual investigations (as is in fact done), that the theology of the Old Testament, in general and in particular, has been taken up into the theology of the New Testament in such a way that they mutually determine and illuminate each other. Thus only a biblical theology can bring into full light of day the fulness of a New Testament theology.

Such a theology of the New Testament has much significance for theology in general. It is of course most fruitful for the discipline out of which it grew, the exegesis of the New Testament. And here it is well to add that there are various reasons why Catholic scientific cooperation on the theology of the New Testament came so relatively late. (Meinertz, introducing his *Theology of the New Testament* in 1954, could say with reason: 'This is the first general presentation of New Testament theology from the Catholic side, that makes any claim to fulness'.) One reason is that even in the nineteenth and the beginning of the twentieth century, Sacred Scripture was rather in the background in Catholic theology. One can adduce the fact that 'Catholic exegesis stood too long on the defensive, and so neglected too much the rich exegetical results of which it could have made use' (A. Bea). One can also emphasize the priority—justifiable in itself—of dogmatic theology, whose structure is so foreign to that of a biblical theology.

But there is another decisive reason, as it appears to me.

For a long time, biblical or New Testament theology felt itself, by reason of origins, to be expressly opposed to Orthodox Protestantism and to its dogmatic theology. This opposition was understood differently during the 'Age of Enlightenment', of 'Idealism', of 'Positivism'. But in any case it marked off biblical theology from the orthodoxy of Protestantism. This polemical attitude, which went back of course to the Reformation principle of *sola scriptura*, went so far in certain circumstances that biblical theology looked on itself as a substitute for dogmatic theology. But the work of biblical theology on the New Testament made it clear that a New Testament theology was to be justified, not by its opposition to Protestantism, but by the necessities of exegesis and dogmatic theology. And only then could the misgivings of Catholic theology be overcome. First came monographies on individual subjects of biblical theology, then partial presentations of biblical theology, and finally general coverage. Biblical or New Testament theology had discovered its objective starting-point.

Exegesis is presupposed by a theology of the New Testament; and exegesis needs such a theology. Without it, exegesis will not for instance easily find the correct basis for the exposition of an individual book of the New Testament. And without it, the work of interpretation easily succumbs to the danger of isolating individual texts from the whole. For instance: if one knows, from a presentation of the theology of the New Testament, St Paul's general attitude toward the Law, one will not miss the fact that his statements in the Epistle to the Galatians are to some extent one-sided. And if one knows the Pauline theology of the Law, one will not be liable to misunderstand the Law as a code of morals or as a past historical situation. This contribution of a theology of the New

Testament to exegesis is also one of the reasons for its existence. In the long run, it came to be because of the *excursus*, added to the commentaries with regard to individual theological concepts and themes, out of which grew monographies. On the other hand, a careful and clear-sighted exegesis will always be able to check critically any theology of the New Testament, as indeed it will always wish to. All New Testament disciplines are in the end at the service of New Testament theology; so too exegesis, the more it penetrates to reality at particular points, the more it will put its results at the disposition of New Testament theology as a whole, and thus help it to launch ever further into the deep.

The 'History of Dogma' as it is called, will also benefit by a theology of the New Testament, for in such history are debated the theological considerations in which the faith of the primitive Church ponders the claims of the foundation of the faith. The faith of the primitive Church is the faith of the Church at its origin, and this, even from the purely historical point of view, is something unique. But its chief distinction is that it remains decisive, as the divinely-constituted and permanent source, for the later development of the truths of faith.

New Testament theology has special significance for dogmatic theology, and so for the theological effort whereby, when the faith of the Church has been collected from all its sources, theological decisions are taken with regard to present-day concepts. Dogmatic theology is not confined to the New Testament as such for its information; it has before it a New Testament which has been illuminated, even with regard to its theological intentions, by an objective development of its theology. When the Bible or the New Testament, as the case may be, has thus been rendered transparent, the dogmatic theologian is forced to a much more radical re-thinking of the truths of faith than he is used to when reading the New Testament merely in the light of his own theological questioning and his own theological answers.

Sacred Scripture, propounded according to its theology, demands for instance of the dogmatic theologian a constantly new effort to pinpoint certain fundamental concepts of faith, as R. Schnackenburg explains in a later essay in this book. It reminds the theologian of the basic Scriptural concepts of the nature of man, which have long fallen into oblivion, and calls for new efforts of discussion. Or it brings up certain fundamental concepts which have often become blurred, such as 'Kingdom of God', 'Saviour', 'Grace' (*Charis*), and forces the theologian to clarify his notions and enunciate their truths more in accordance with the primary and objective sense. It urges dogmatic theology to take some theological notion and work it out more deeply than hitherto by showing its presence and proportion in the totality of New Testament theology. What 'Glory' (*Doxa*) means, for instance, precisely when considered in the context of its manifold shades of meaning, is as yet relatively virgin soil to dogma.

And the theology of the New Testament can also put before dogmatic theology certain comprehensive themes, in whose theological explanation the biblical foundations have hitherto counted far too little. For instance, what the theology of the New Testament has been working out with regard to 'History as a process of salvation' or 'Eschatology', or the sacramental foundations of the new life and so on, will surely affect the dogmatic explanations. It is well known, for instance, that what has been worked out with regard to the Church has already borne fruit for theology, and even for the authentic decisions of the teaching authority. The gaps that may be noticed in dogmatic theology will also be pointed out by a New Testament theology. Must not dogmatic theology begin to consider, in all its ramifications, what the 'Word of God' implies as a means of salvation, and ask itself in what sense it is a means of salvation?

Finally, a thoroughgoing presentation of the theology of the New Testament, especially as a whole, is a challenge to the dogmatic theologian to investigate and check the formal structure of theology as a whole. Dogma is unchangeable, but that does not imply that the outlines of dogmatic theology are unchangeable. It must think over anew the process of its presentation, which is not merely conventional or technical, if biblical theology on the whole shows a general structure so different from that of dogmatic theology. After all, biblical theology is not merely the theology of the original faith of the Church. It is also the theology of the inspired scriptural testimony, and therefore the main source of dogmatics. There are signs that dogmatic theology is already taking up the duties imposed on it by the theology of the New Testament (though not by it alone), as is shown by the new outline of theology offered for instance by Karl Rahner.

Thus the theology of the New Testament, expressly or otherwise, puts many urgent questions to dogmatic theology. But this is not from any secret, perhaps unconscious will to replace dogmatic theology by its own elaborations, nor from any desire to make itself the norm of dogmatic theology. It is still aware of the fact that theological knowledge is finally won, by theological means, in dogmatic theology and finds expression there. For dogmatic theology, based on Scripture and Tradition (no matter how one determines their relationship more closely), has to think out the whole deposit of faith in the Church and bring it forward in present-day concepts.

But the theology of the New Testament also knows, from an experience gained gradually in painful and often controversial work, what radical and pure power of thought, what riches of basic theological insight and wisdom is given to the Church in the Sacred Scripture, and especially in the New Testament. It strives, in its own place, to serve dogmatic theology and indeed the Church's thinking in general, by casting light on theology in so far as it is attainable in Scripture, particularly in the New Testament, and bringing thereto an expert and immediate knowledge. 'Sacred Scripture cannot be too highly estimated', says St Bonaventure when discussing the place of its study in theology.

What has been said here does not exhaust the significance of a theology of the New Testament. But to indicate its uses in the preaching and catechism of the Church—and even in its controversies—would take us too far afield.

Eduard
Schillebeeckx, O.P.

EXEGESIS, DOGMATICS AND
THE DEVELOPMENT OF DOGMA

The religion of revelation is essentially a dialogue, a meeting between man and the living God. That sounds indeed like a modern 'existentialist' catch-word, a fashionable phrase to be used on every occasion, suitable or not. A certain amount of courage is sometimes needed to write it down once more. However it is in reality only another and a modern word for a reality which has always been recognized by the life of religion, namely the personal relationship to God, based on grace or on the personal call of God, which expresses itself in theological terms.

If we take the words 'meeting with God' and 'experience of God' in their proper sense, they are a definition of our heavenly vision of God and not of our human life of grace. Here below, in our life of religion, we can really speak only of an experience of faith and love. But from this and in this, the consciousness of being graciously addressed by God—mediated to us subjectively—makes possible an exchange of personal relations with God, in faith. But this remains always a matter of faith, since in this fellowship with God in grace there is no objective (or perceptible) mediation of consciousness. To put it more exactly, the real exchange of personal relationship between God and man which grace makes possible is a partnership in which God addresses man personally and man answers God personally in faith. Thus it is a meeting with God in faith, which is the modern and correct expression for the dogma of grace.

Faith is man's answer to the self-disclosure of the living God. To approach another being in true intimacy is something which depends on the nature of the being in question, and can therefore take place on different levels.

'In principle, every being lies open and accessible to every other. But material things in a way other than that of the spirit and of man, and God in yet a different way. Material things possess no inwardness, no personal mystery. They are at the disposition of the spirit of man as he investigates and masters them. Hence we never speak in this connexion of "meeting" with things, with plants or beasts. Man, of his own power, can take hold of them.

'With spiritual beings the matter is quite different. Because of their freedom, they are the source of what they themselves really are: they have, or rather, they are a personal mystery, to which one cannot have free access from without. In their inwardness, they are accessible to others only in so far as they freely lay themselves open and disclose themselves. A spirit grants knowledge of itself. The more fully he can dispose of himself, as a free person, the more will his laying himself open to others be a free gift of a love freely bestowed, an act of confident self-communication. Thus does the other truly meet a fellow-person. And such a meeting is possible only within the framework of a "forthcomingness", a confidential self-disclosure on the one side, and a receptive, hearkening response of dedication on the other.

'If we speak of men, things become more complicated. Every relationship between men takes place by means of the corporal element. It is this element which lays the human person open to the outward world, and hence it must be that the free personal possession of man is something limited. The body reveals, but it also conceals the secret of the human person. This means that on the one hand, a human being, whether he will it or not, is open and accessible to his fellow-men. His bodily form betrays his inward self. On the other hand, however, he reveals himself only in freedom, precisely because the origins of his bodily expression are to a certain extent free acts.

'A personal meeting between men cannot, therefore, take the direction of an effort to master what in the other is involuntary "bodily" self-utterance. That would reduce a man to the level of an object. A truly human meeting can only take place when the human person opens up freely to another who accepts the confidence of this revelation. Every self-willed approach to one's fellow-men is the exclusion, the disregard of the human personality and can therefore not be a personal meeting. For the one who imposes himself on the other reaches only what is not typically personal in him. The mystery of his real life remains concealed. And that is why, in every human meeting, revelation and faith are exchanged between man and man. Only in the realm of love does this revelation and this faith attain their full stature.

'Finally, God. He is the absolute source of his inner mystery. He is a person in the perfectly absolute meaning of the word—and for that very reason, though to us incomprehensibly, in the unity of three persons. It is in this understanding that revelation and faith, which are the constitutive elements of true meeting with God, receive for the first time their true significance. The notion of "meeting with God" contains a reference to our experience of natural existence. Without this human meaning of meeting within the world, the theological concept, given us by faith, of "meeting with God", of "revelation" (which means unveiling), and of faith would be empty words for us'. (See E. Schillebeeckx, *Christ, the Sacrament of Man's Meeting With God,* Mainz, 1960.)

Creation, in which God reveals himself indirectly so to speak, does give us the means of opening up a perspective in which the absolute reality of God is recognized as a mystery. But the precise form of this mystery is only shown to us in the history of salvation, culminating in the manifestation, the Epiphany, of the Son of God as man among us. When man in faith answers God who reveals himself, his response has an essential relation to this objective revelation or self-disclosure of God. No statement can therefore be made about the structure of the act of faith without an essential co-relationship to the content of revelation. Act of faith and object of faith both are based on a grace which, as it were, holds together this essential connexion between act of faith and object of faith by means of a connaturality of spirit between us and the reality of salvation. This spiritual kinship is a gift from God, given with the light of faith, and embraces the real process which makes contact with us in history and, above all, in the historical reality of Christ.

There is thus a double unity, of the inward and the outward, and it has further a basis in the structure of man. All human activity is marked by the way of being in which humanity must live. The material world, existence in the world, are the only gates man has whereby to come to articulate consciousness of any field of knowledge. We only know what exists as matter. Non-material things we know only in so far as they have some relationship with the material; so we know our self and others in so far as we and they exist in the world, and we know God only in so far as he is creator of all these things, or in so far as he graciously manifests himself in this world, namely in the process of salvation. All human activity is therefore marked by its being directed outward, and by its inward spiritual element, an inner appeal, which animates and inspires our human actions in and upon the world.

Faith, though only realized in grace, is therefore truly a human act, made what it is by the nature of humanity. So the act of faith is understandable by means of its being directed 'outward' towards the world of men and things, where at a given date Christ appeared, founding a church; and it is also understandable by means of its inwardness. There is an aspect of 'interiority' in which, for all the constant outwardness, an inward, spiritual, gracious appeal is experienced at the same time. It is the divine invitation, calling us to the personal initiative of dedication in faith, and inspiring us thereto, precisely with regard to the element of public revelation which confronts us. In the grace of faith, God bestows upon us a spiritual kinship precisely with the reality which we meet as we live in and experience the salvific process.

We must always keep before us these two elements of faith, especially when we put the problem of the highly divergent stand-points from which faith looks out when its thinking is exegetical or biblical, and when it is dogmatic.

Faith includes an element of consciousness and knowledge. But not any sort of knowledge. In the Christian faith, the knowledge we speak of comes from being addressed. This call evokes a hearing. Revelation and faith form together a dialogue between man and the living God. Such a structure is verified not only in revelation when completed or constituted, but also in the faith which goes out to the process of revelation itself, while still open. For the process takes place precisely in the form of dialogue. In the relationship of dialogue, and through this relationship between the Jewish people and Yahweh, in loyal obedience or in rebellion, God gradually unfolds his plan of salvation. Revelation comes to life because God is not only the creator who creates and moves man's history, but because he is also—and formally—the God of salvation who manifests himself in action, coming to grips with the freedom of man which is the stuff of history. It is in history that God brings about what he has set before himself in his care for the salvation of man. And he does it in such a way that his action on behalf of the salvation of man is visible in history in a veiled manner.

The action of God in saving man is itself revelation. It is revealed as it becomes history, and it becomes history in so far as it reveals itself. Thus revelation is a process of growth which came to its final form in Christ and the early apostolic Church. The Old Testament, under the aspect of religious faith, possesses a certain independent value. But in the end this Old Testament revelation must be seen as the pre-history of the Christian revelation, as the process of growth into the mystery of Christ who is the centre and the *telos*, the final end, of the whole revelation. The whole salvific history of the Old Testament is directed to this final stage so that, ultimately, the first word of revelation can only be fully understood in the light of the final stage of the definitive revelation.

Though revelation primarily consists of the salvific action of God, this salvific history only attains its full significance as revelation when it is perceived by the people of God. This means a grasp of history which is the fruit of grace. From its consciousness of salvation, from its sense of being the people of God, Israel begins to understand and interpret its history as the action of God on his people. God's way of salvation is a divine action, but it is at the same time a divine interpretation of this action, namely by the prophetic word. This word throws light on the presence and on the import of God's process of salvation. God does not just say something *about* our salvation; he accomplishes it in history. But the meaning of history he must again himself interpret for us in the prophetic word. 'First however it must be known, that no prophecy of Scripture comes by private interpretation' (2 Pt 1 : 20; see also Amos 3 : 7; Is 42 : 9).

Revelation by deed and revelation by word are the pillars of the revealed religion. But that is not all. The history of religions has taught us that a community which claims to have been founded on some fact of history, and maintains itself historically on these grounds, almost necessarily gives this fact value by means of 'the Book' or its own 'Scripture', at least to some extent. This element of human culture was introduced by God as an essential element into the revealed religion. By way of popular traditions, themselves already depositories of the people of God's sense of salvation and religious attitude to history, the Sacred Scripture arose. In Sacred Scripture the people of God learn to know explicitly of its divine election, and of how this call came. And in listening to the prophetic words, it understands and constitutes itself as the people of God. This very way in which God wills to bring his people into being is the way he chose for its constitutive elements, of which Sacred Scripture is one. As a matter of fact, Karl Rahner sees here the very basis of scriptural inspiration (see K. Rahner, *Inspiration in the Bible* [New York: Herder and Herder, 1961]).

The salvific history, the word, the Sacred Scripture, form only one single continuous activity of grace, which appears to us in historical and comprehensible form. In it the following elements of structure can be recognized. Firstly, God's saving acts are realized in the history of Israel, in the form of a visible life of fellowship with God. In the field of religion, this history of Israel expresses itself in the growing sense of salvation possessed by the community, and through an understanding of this event which was the gift of grace. The community gradually came to know itself in its supernatural constitution, a process which took place first in tradition, which presents the work of God in the community in an ever-widening perspective and makes the people responsible for its own supernatural realization. In this tradition, Yahweh expresses himself as the word of God, and finally God will put his seal on it in Sacred Scripture, with the guarantee—inspiration—that such an expression of himself is the faithful mirror of his decree of salvation as he willed to have it realized in his people. (See, among others, L. Cerfaux, *La parole de Dieu*, Louvain, 1959: 'In fact, inspiration in the theological sense which this word has when applied to the Bible, is not a completely new intervention, complete in itself. It continues a movement, brings it to perfection and has its own *raison d'être* in the origin of this movement'.) The same structure of tradition and fixing in writing is verifiable also in the New Testament revelation, though of course here the process was gone through in a much shorter time.

We may not then regard Sacred Scripture as the whole of the revealed religion of Christianity. But it is still an essential, fundamental, constitutive and irreplaceable element. Scripture belongs to the constitution of the Church as it was instituted by Christ, with its apostolic offices, its living preaching voice, and its sacraments. It is therefore part of the fundamental structure of the apostolic Church, part of the *depositum fidei*, the deposit of faith, by which the post-apostolic Church is always guided. From this point of view the Church, and therefore the magisterium, the teaching authorities, are given their norms by Sacred Scripture. And there is no contradiction in saying that it is a truth of faith that the ecclesiastical teaching authority is the final instance in judging the interpretation of Scripture. The guarantee for correct exegesis lies with the Church, thanks to its apostolic *charisma*, or grace. The teaching office is the immediate norm for our faith, but this teaching office is itself guided by the primitive apostolic Church and thus by the Scriptures. Nourishing itself on the Bible, and living from the Bible and from the reality of salvation, the Church gives the norms for our faith, our exegesis, and for our thinking out the faith, that is, dogmatics.

From all this it follows that without exegesis and biblical theology no dogmatics is possible. But the correct relationship between the two is not that dogmatics searches the Scriptures for 'proof texts' for its own theses. On the contrary, Christian exegesis and biblical theology have also a critical function with regard to present-day theses of dogmatic theology. It is true that dogma is not confined to Scripture for its source, but in every instance Scripture remains, in its quality of special primary archive of the consciousness of the Church, an inviolable norm for all theological activity, even though reading of the Scripture must take place in and with the Church, of which it is the Sacred Scripture. Looked at in this way, dogmatics implies Christian exegesis and biblical theology.

On the other hand, however, dogmatics is more than exegesis, more than theology of the Bible. The content of faith is all that is contained in the salvific call of God to man. By means of the salvific process and its biblical self-utterance, under the guard of the Church's teaching office, the word of God in the Church is directed to all mankind, and hence also to the men of the present day. What is heard must, then, constantly be brought anew into relationship with any given moment of the spiritual situation of men as they listen here and now to the Word of God. The hearing of the one word of God is subject to the conditions of each age, as Sacred Scripture itself already shows. And this reception is so intimately connected with revelation that each present-day's utterance of what has been heard coincides, to some extent, with revelation itself. The definition of a dogma of faith, in spite of the novelty of its formulation in comparison with a biblical statement, is indeed a way of rendering the original word of revelation. For instance, when the Council of Chalcedon expresses the reality of the salvation present in Christ by the words, 'Two natures, one person', the believing community hears therein what the Apostles heard as they hearkened to the reality of Christ.

And yet the way in which the one word of God is made one's own is different. This appropriation belongs however to dogma. It is the dogma itself. A dogma is the correct, though never exhaustive, hearing of a reality of revelation or of a word of revelation. (And this is what gives rise to the immense difference between the development of faith and theological development.)

We give the name of Tradition precisely to *the way and manner in which* Scripture and revelation are heard ever anew by man, *the maker of history*. Tradition is nothing else but the abiding, always actual, grace-inspired hearing of the reality of revelation, which found its constitutive depository in the apostolic Church with its Scripture. We maintain therefore, with some exegetes, that Scripture has so to speak a double context: its own biblical context, to be sounded by the exegete and biblical theologian; and the context of every period of Church history. Thus Scripture has, we may say, the contemporary context, which is investigated by the dogmatic theologian and which is connected with what is called the development of dogma. It should be emphasized that this is not a question of trying to find the later dogma *as such* in Sacred Scripture. Not infrequently every such reading of Scripture necessarily involved reading something into Scripture, an eis-egesis not an ex-egesis.

But the word of God, attested in Scripture, is directed to the hearing not only of the Jewish people and the primitive apostolic Church, but to the men of every age as well. The exegete tries to establish how this word of God was pronounced to the Jewish people and the early Church, and how it was heard by them. The dogmatic theologian, on the contrary, tries to ascertain how the self-same word, already heard by Israel and the apostolic Church and yet directed to us in the twentieth century, may be heard by us without distortion. In such an investigation one will start with a clear idea of how God spoke to Israel and to the primitive Church, and one knows how the latter understood and followed the word of God. Thus once again, there is no theology or dogmatics without exegesis and biblical theology. What was heard in Old Testament and apostolic times belongs in fact to the constitutive phase of revelation. Hence it is a once-for-all, an unrepeatable event, which will remain the norm for the obedient ear of the post-apostolic Church. For this reason, exegesis has the place of honour in all theological thinking of the faith.

On the other hand the voice of God, in spite of public revelation having come to an end, remains always an *actual* reality. The revelation of God in Christ is in truth the personal self-presentation of the living God, who gives himself to be intimately known and experienced in a personal gesture in which he comes to meet man and invites him to a life of fellowship with himself. Hence, as we have said, the salvific reality of revelation contains, since it is directed to us, not only the historically fixed points of God's saving acts, with their prophetic explanation—the so-called 'public revelation'—but also an inner call of God through the grace of faith or the 'light of faith'. And it is through the latter that we can personally perceive with our hearts and accept God's gracious offer of salvation.

Sacred Scripture itself has expressed this by the words, 'the anointing by the Holy Spirit', as I. de la Potterie has recently proved in a careful study. (See his 'L'onction du chrétien par la foi' *Biblica*, 1959, in which he propounds the biblical foundations for the Thomistic doctrine of 'the light of faith'.) This anointing, or chrism, is the word of Christ itself, the 'faith that comes by hearing', in so far as the Holy Spirit brings it to our mind. It is the *locutio interna*, the inner speech, which goes with the *fides ex auditu*, the external word heard from the preaching Church. Both are bound up with one another, the internal anointing and the external hearing. When therefore one hears in the Church the word of God, one may see it as having, so to speak, a horizontal and a vertical dimension. In faith, there is an inner confrontation with God who gives testimony to himself here and now, really and actually; and there is at the same time an *Anamnesis*, an evocation in memory, of what Sacred Scripture and Tradition affirm about this utterance of God. This biblical doctrine of the 'Anointing by the Spirit' was taken up by the Fathers, and after their example, by the great theologians of the Middle Ages, e.g. St Thomas, and explained similarly as 'an inner, divine instinct which invites us to believe'. (See St Thomas, *Commentary on St John*, c. 6, lect. 5; *Summa*, II–II, q 2, a. 9 ad 3.) Earlier Church councils too spoke of 'an inner impulse and an inner illumination' (see Denzinger, 178, 1791).

God's gracious intervention in history, which reached its climax in the person and life of the God-man, is thus made understandable for us men by the public word of the inspired prophets, and finally by the word of Christ himself. Scripture gives us an inspired account of all this; and then, to complete the process, comes the grace of faith, to open the heart of each of the faithful for the divine contents and meaning of this revelation. One of the fathers of the Council of Trent alluded to this reality of grace when he said: 'Because the Son of God was not to abide by us permanently in the flesh, he sent the Holy Spirit, who will reveal the mysteries of God to the heart of believers, and *every day*, to the end of time, will instruct the Church in all truth, and contend against the eventual doubts which are to arise in the hearts of men' (Council of Trent, Acts, V 11, XII 508). Separated from the public revelation, the inner grace of faith or the 'inward voice of God' would not have expression, and the word of God could not be heard. But on the other hand, hearing the external, public revelation without the inward light of faith could not possibly bring about a true dedication in faith to the word, and the word of God would not be perceived in its divine import.

From this it follows that the faith of the Church has as its norm the historical event of Israel and of Jesus, as testified to in the Scriptures. And at the same time this faith is the result of the *actual*, present, self-revelation of the heavenly Christ *through* his Spirit in the Church.

This means that dogmatics, if it is to listen to the word of God and hear it in its purity, must first study Scripture, and then past Tradition. But since the same word of God is still being addressed to us also, the dogmatic theologian will put questions to the Scriptures and to Tradition which the exegete or the historian would not. The biblical theologian and the exegete ask themselves: What does Israel think, under the divine inspiration, of itself as people of God, and of Yahweh as the God of Israel? What does Christ think of himself and of man? What does the primitive Church think, when confronted with the risen Christ, of itself and of Christ? The dogmatic theologian takes all this for granted and goes further.

Not that he wants to prolong Christian exegesis in human, philosophical thinking, and erect a superstructure on what the Christian exegete, under the guidance of the Church, has heard from this divine call. But the dogmatic theologian takes as his norm what Israel and the apostolic Church have heard of the word of God and tries, in his role of a present-day believer, to listen to the word of God

as it addresses his contemporary situation. He is a sacred
contemplative whose attention is given, so to speak, to
trying to hear in a new way, with every intrinsic relationship it can possess, the self-same word of God, and so to
formulate it for his own times. There is nothing new
therefore, and yet everything is different. And this shows
the difference in perspective between the Christian theologian and the exegete. Yet at the same time all this brings
about the connexion between the results of Christian
exegesis and theology, precisely because hearkening to the
word of God in grace, which is faith, creates the identity
between Scripture and dogma, Scripture and tradition,
Scripture and a theology guided by the Church. The result
is not a superstructure but a meditation on the word of
God as it has been heard.

Properly speaking, there is absolutely no difference in
stand-point between the Christian exegete and the dogmatic theologian. It would be wrong to think that the
exegete stood outside the faith of the Church and studied
the text of the Bible in the way an expert studies profane
literature. There is indeed a difference between pure
biblical criticism, literary and philological exegesis, and
Christian exegesis, even though despite the radical difference in stand-point, they all use the same methods of
criticism. Like the theologian, the exegete hearkens to
Sacred Scripture as an enquirer who believes. As for the
theologian, so for the Christian exegete, the subordination
of critical reason to the light of faith is the stand-point from
which he tries to grasp the word of God. In scholastic
terminology, we could say that the *lumen quo*, the light
by which Christian biblical scholarship reads, is the same
as that of theology or dogmatics. The two, exegesis and
theology, are critical sciences. And both are sciences of the

9

faith, which address themselves to the critical faculties. Further, from the point of view of the matter to be studied under this same light, these two sciences of faith have the same field, the word of God in revelation as it is heard and accepted in the reaction of man who believes.

All the same—and here is the formal difference—the aspect under which the believing exegete hears and searches, systematizes and synthetizes the divine word of revelation, is different from the particular aspect under which the theologian, in his faith's intelligence, studies the same word of revelation and does his work of synthetizing it according to its interior articulations. The Christian exegete and biblical theologian investigate the word of God as it is given them in its exact biblical context, and as it was heard by the Old Testament people of God and the early apostolic Church. Hence too the way he appeals to human reason will be other than that of the theologian. His primary interest is to establish positively a given, set type of thinking out the faith, as for instance the theology of St. Paul; his interest is not the speculative reasoning or structure (*ratio*).

The theologian, on the other hand, investigates the same word of God, but from the point of view of how it addresses men of all ages, and how it must be hearkened to here and now. And we could say more concretely: as it addresses us, the men of our times. This criterion, the relationship to the present day, 'in so far as it addresses us, the men of our times', I add not from any impulse toward up-to-date subjectivism, but because we know that God does not speak to 'Man' as such, to an abstraction called humanity, but to men in the concrete, involved in history. He speaks to men of biblical times, to men of the ancient Church of the Fathers, to men of the Middle Ages, to modern men, to men to-day. This does not reduce the word of God to something merely 'relative', valid for one age but not for another. In faith man, the real man as he exists in every epoch of time, always seeks to reach the objective content of the revealed word of God. But no matter how absolute and unchangeable is the supernatural truth, it—like every other truth—still shares, in the form it reaches our minds, the qualities of all human things. It has the imperfection, the relativity, the possibility of development, the historical conditioning which goes with all truth as possessed by men. One and the same perception of the mind can be illuminated and approached from different sides, so that in one and the same reality different, mutually complementary but correct insights are possible.

Such perspectives with regard to truth are essential to all human knowledge. We meet them in the Scriptures themselves, for we rightly speak of the 'Synoptic', the 'Johannine', the 'Pauline' picture of Christ. And the eschatological views of the Johannine writings differ from those of the Pauline. And so on. The theologian will listen to Scripture and tradition; he will decipher the many ecclesiastical reflexions on the word of revelation as they came to life in the course of centuries; he will attend to the present preaching of the Church and the present tendencies of the Church. And thus he will try to hear the same word of God ever more adequately, though always to a relative extent, for by his very work he always leaves further work to coming generations. He will try to hear the word in its totality, to organize it according to its intrinsic articulations, so that it can address concretely, in present and future preaching, the present and future generations.

Hence the theologian's appeal to 'reason' is rather an

appeal to speculative reason, while the exegete rather relies on the application of the critical faculty to the factual. But one must not misunderstand these expressions, as sometimes happens. Speculative reason does not mean the ability to add another ingredient to the data, but the power to grasp the data in their meaningful reality, seeing their intrinsic relationships within the faith and their mutual connexions, as for instance St Paul himself already tried to do. What a St Paul could do, though of course he had the guarantee of inspiration and was a vehicle of the constitutive revelation which was not yet closed, the dogmatic theologian does also, but in a purely scientific and therefore fallible way. He tries to penetrate more deeply into the meaning of the realities of salvation given him to study. He tries to trace their mutual connexions and their bearing on the salvation of living men. He strives to throw light on their meaning by means of human analogies.

The objection can be made against many contributions from exegetes and biblical theologians, that in keeping with their task and their scientific quality, they render exactly and correctly the convictions and ideas of the biblical authors, but, perhaps unconsciously, they propose this description as something normative, neglecting the critical elements which are needed in dogmatics, and which are at the disposal of dogmatics only when theology is not just biblical but theology as such. For theology takes counsel not only with the Bible, though first of all there, but with Church life and thought as it grew out of the Bible in the course of Church history. For instance: one is not finished with what faith teaches about the angels when, by means of an exact biblical theology, one has garnered the doctrine of the New Testament about the angels. Likewise, one is not done with the revealed doctrine about

Mary when the biblical picture of Mary has been neatly and clearly drawn.

However, a similar objection may be made against many dogmatic theologians. Their search for 'proof-texts' from the Bible on behalf of a dogmatic theology which is already cut and dried can hardly be called a theological procedure. Within the development there is an identity between the word of God to which Scripture testifies, and the word of God which is defined dogmatically. Hence in the Scripture itself there must be an objective dynamism, a real expansive tendency, which cannot be established by literary and philological methods, but only by Christian exegesis and dogmatics. We do not mean thereby that we make St Paul or St John say what the Church now says in full expressiveness. But we show in the Scriptures the 'limits of the Pauline thought', or of the Johannine thought, as they appear from the stand-point of later dogmas. These limits, as has been rightly said, are not purely negative. They rather indicate an incompleteness, a start, a tendency—or, as has been said, 'they are realities on the march'.

On these profound realities of Scripture rests the so-called *Sensus Plenior*, the fuller sense of the Old Testament, that is, its Christian meaning, as does the full sense of the New Testament. The latter, though perhaps not identical in expression with later dogmas, has still an intrinsic connexion with this dogmatic development. For through the light of faith we ourselves stand in direct contact with the *reality* of Christ and the whole mystery of salvation, and not merely with a biblical account *of* this reality. The truth is never formally comprised in a book or a word but in the Spirit, who speaks in the writer and lives in the hearer. The divine revelation, as it is offered to us in Scripture and Tradition, can only be perceived by the heart, when God himself, through the light of faith, brings its meaning to light in our hearts. If then he who inspires dogmas, the Spirit namely of Christ in the formulations of the Church, is also the author of Scripture, even though it be in the form of human words conditioned by their times, it is clear that the first, the biblical utterance of the Holy Spirit in any given case, will have an intrinsic relationship with the later word, which the Holy Spirit brings to utterance in dogma, with regard to the same reality of salvation. That this divine word is expressed in human terms demands, as does every other serious study of texts, the historical, philological and literary method, as indeed the encyclical *Divino Afflante Spiritu* insists so forcefully.

But the divine quality of this word escapes these methods. It can only be heard if the critical method is taken up into the light of faith, which sympathizes and feels at one with the reality of salvation. The intentions of the Holy Spirit 'who spoke through the prophets', surpasses what the sacred writers with their limited powers could express. But for all their limitations, they express deliberately, if only vaguely, something of what the Holy Spirit really meant, and what is brought to clearer expressiveness in the definition of a dogma.

To be sure, it is one of the tasks of the Christian exegete to warn the dogmatic theologian time after time not to undertake to read things into Scripture. The Christian exegete, for instance, will first of all and as far as possible establish the exact peculiarities of the thought of St Paul. He will do this by marking off this thought from what other sacred writers, later theologians, and even dogma have said about one and the same proposition of faith. But on the other hand, revelation is one single whole, which goes beyond the particular synthesis of each individual sacred writer. Even if we take the whole of the express synthesis of all the sacred writers together—a totality which is the particular theme of what is called 'biblical theology' in contrast to exegesis—still, the divine quality of the word transcends even this. For even in Scripture, the word is expressed only in a human way, and therefore possesses a prophetic expandibility, whose meaning can only gradually be approached through the life of the Church as lived throughout its history.

The divinity of this word, though it is uttered only in the manner of a human word, is precisely the foundation of the 'full sense' which goes with the 'literal sense' of the Bible, or better, is identical with it. This explains why it is necessary in every case to look for the 'full sense' in the development of the 'literal sense', as known by philology and literary criticism. If there is a gap between them, we are no longer dealing with a 'fuller sense' but possibly with a typological one (in a broad sense) or even with an 'accommodated sense'. This results from the structure of the divine word, as it is found incorporated in the human. Just as Christ is God in his humanity, and thus is God the Son in a human way, so too the word of Scripture has a theandric, divinely human quality. The human meaning, recognizable to the exegete, is human precisely in its divinity. This human word contains a 'plus', something extra, an objective dynamism whose meaning comes to be recognized in the Church only by a laborious process. It is only through the light of faith that we have spiritual kinship with the divineness of this word. For instance, we must make vital contact with the reality of the faith itself, and not merely with the biblical doctrine about this reality if, as we read, we are to derive a deeper meaning from the presence of Mary under the cross, and at the Pentecostal event in the Coenaculum.

This meaning is not arrived at by merely 'profane' exegesis. If it is to be found, it must undoubtedly be by what must be called 'Christian exegesis'. Only in such exegesis is it possible to recognize in the texts that, although the New Testament writers did not yet know of later dogmas as they were to be expressed in the Church, they put into their writings a certain objective dynamism, or tendency, which points on darkly toward what will be heard by the Church, clearly and expressively, as the word of God. To keep to the same example: we see in the Scriptures how obviously Mary is given the value of an ecclesiastical figure in the Book of Revelation and in the Fourth Gospel. So much so, that what is primarily intended, namely the 'Woman-Church', is as it were combined in one perspective with the 'Woman-Mary'. And we observe further that in the gospel of the Infancy also, the Old Testament themes of the indwelling of God in the People of God, or the Old Testament Church, are the prisms through which one looks for the reality of 'Mary the Mother of Jesus'. Thus it becomes clear to the Christian exegete and to the dogmatic theologian that the distance between the Marian dogmas of the Church and the biblical picture of Mary is not so great as one had thought. The mere fact that the Old Testament idea of the eschatological indwelling of God in the 'Daughter of Sion' and in the holy city of Jerusalem is transferred to Mary by the New Testament, even though often by a mere hint, is enough to lend these seemingly simple biblical references to Mary a deeper meaning, which come to clear consciousness in the Church only in the course of centuries.

This objective dynamism in the meaning of the Bible,

the so-called *sensus plenior,* fuller sense, is really a meaning belonging to the Bible, and not just a *sensus consequens,* a consequence drawn from biblical meanings. This may be shown once more from the same example. Certain traits of the 'Daughter of Sion' are in fact attributed to Mary and others not. The Church is therefore conscious of a difference. This indicates that the Church, in making this distinction, is itself guided by the dynamic which is really and objectively present in the Scripture itself, and recognizes this dynamism as the divinity of the human biblical word.

Church dogmas are not formally theological deductions from New Testament data. They are not a *sensus consequens,* which indeed could not in itself be called a *sensus scripturisticus,* or a meaning given by Scripture. Rather, dogmas have an intrinsic connexion with the 'fuller sense' of the Scriptures, being the unfolding of what was already present—vaguely—in the apostolic consciousness, of which the Sacred Scriptures are the written record.

As the process of unfolding this kernel goes on, theological thinking has undoubtedly an irreplaceable function within the life of faith of the Church and under her teaching authority. This gives rise to the impression that dogmas are part of the *sensus consequens,* but this would be to misrepresent the psychological structure of the process of human thought. For psychologically, discursive thought is nothing else than the totality of experimental knowledge itself, that is, experience constantly growing but dominated by the total object which from the beginning was implicitly also part of consciousness. In the process of explicit proof, one sees the original data in the light of implications which have been discovered both by reflexion and by experimental knowledge. These implications may

appear as consequences, but they had been present, un-
noticed, in the consciousness from the start. Thus development is always a passage from implicit to explicit
consciousness, and not the passage from a recognized principle to a fully new truth, deduced by a purely logical
process and in no way present in the consciousness at the
beginning.

This holds good for the knowledge given by faith, if
this is indeed a knowledge which comes from being addressed. If it did not, we could not see how the so-called
'New Truths', the dogmas, are revealed by God and are
therefore to be accepted on his authority.

A *locutio attestans*, a divinely attested utterance, is of
its nature also a search for an active, responsive reaction
by man to the definite enunciation which God imparts.
It is the summons to the obedience of faith. In some way
or other, that which is formally revealed must have been
perceived in apostolic times. The appeal which is contained in the divine testimony as such can never be reduced to an invitation to deduce consequences. It must be
an invitation to faith, or as E. Dhanis says (*Gregorianum*,
1953) a call for belief. That all real developments in the
faith, that all later dogmas must from the beginning be
attested by the impressive voice of God which invites us
to faith is a necessary consequence of the closing of 'the
deposit of faith'. But since the Christian message is addressed to the men of all ages and not merely to those of
the apostolic times, and since in fact the message originally
heard must be constantly translated and transformed anew
into expressions which put what was said into relation
with the present-day, ever-changing situation of mankind,
it is to be expected *a priori* that revelation will attest
certain aspects formally, but in such a way that these

truths, formally imparted, are attested merely by means of suggestion.

Only when a new set of problems is posed do the different aspects of truth come to the consciousness of the Church and find recognition in their quality of formally revealed truths. We may use a natural analogy to illustrate this, though the comparison is not exact. When a professor in an oral examination wishes to help a student find the answer for which he is struggling in vain, he suggests the answer, but without saying it directly. None the less, he intends to impart formally what in fact he merely suggests. What he says expressly, even though it indicates what he really means only at the level of suggestion, is the means whereby the student finds the truth in question. It would be quite different if the student established another truth, by means of deduction, from a truth which the professor formally uttered, if what the student found were logically connected with it but not intended by the professor. In both cases the discursive intellect is at work. But each case is completely different.

We have something similar in revelation. Theological deduction may well have its part to play, it may indeed be necessary, but only the reaction of faith, on the part of the whole community, can tell whether the truth derived by deduction is really revealed by God. And in the final analysis only the teaching office of the Church is competent to guarantee infallibly the reaction of the believing community. Thus, whatever be the occasions which stimulated and directed the attention of the believing community, perhaps over centuries, the later dogmas stem truly from the original deposit of faith of which the Scriptures speak.

For this reason we find it theologically impossible to

agree with those who maintained, as the formal definition of the Immaculate Conception approached, that there was no need to find this truth either explicitly or implicitly in Scripture, nor indeed even in Tradition in any form whatsoever. Such a tendency is described in V. Sardi's *Solenne Definizione del dogma dell'Immacolata Conceptione*, Roma, 1904-5. What is indisputably correct in this thesis is that, from the apologetic point of view, we are not at all obliged to be able to trace clearly the dogmas of the Church from Scripture all the way through tradition to the present day. That would be impossible.

But all the same, since the Church receives no new revelations, one must be able to show one way or another that the later dogmas really come from the deposit of faith, which was closed long ago, and that they have not merely been added to it. There is no need to demonstrate an explicit continuity. But human psychology contains much more than merely 'explicit knowledge'. Thus God let the sacred writers view Mary, for instance, under the unheard-of traits of the ideal 'Daughter of Sion', which had never been realized by Israel. Thereby he formally *suggested*, precisely by means of these traits of which the apostolic times were conscious, the later Marian dogmas. These are therefore formally and not just virtually *revealed*.

This same principle, that there is a divine quality in the human word of revelation in spite of its being historically conditioned in the manner of utterance, will help us to shed light on the 'fuller sense' of *Old* Testament texts. The particular, direct meaning of these texts is not 'Christian'. They have their own proper meaning for the Jewish people. But let us place these texts in the context of the whole plan of salvation, which finds its fulness in Christ. We know then that the first word of the Old Testament gains its final significance only in the light of Christ's fulfilment, as propounded in the New Testament. Thus it is obvious that the 'literal sense' of the Old Testament is sustained by an objective dynamism, which by means of a particular Jewish meaning still points on to the Christ who comes.

Christ himself said: 'Everything which is written of me in the Law of Moses, in the Prophets and the Psalms, must be fulfilled' (Lk 24:44). Scripture speaks of the disciples' minds 'being opened' so that they could understand the Old Testament Scriptures. According to the first epistle of St Peter (1 Pt 1: 10–12) all that is written in the Old Testament is in the final instance written for us Christians, without prejudice to its particular, independent and Old Testament meaning. With face unveiled we Christians gaze upon the glory of the Lord in the Old Testament (2 Cor 3: 14 ff).

It must be conceded that in the course of Church history the 'fuller sense' was less sought after than the typological sense of the most diverse Old Testament events, a process indulged in with an exuberance, especially in patristic and medieval times, worthy of a Claudel. But 'an abuse does not eliminate a good use'. Scripture remains a living book for all believers. In Old Testament times, after the exile of the sixth century B.C., it was read and re-read constantly in the light of new experiences and in the light of an expectation of the Messiah which grew ever more tense. Thus, for instance, many psalms written perhaps in earlier times gained in messianic clarity as they were sung and prayed in the synagogue services. The ancient Greek translation of the Old Testament, the pre-Christian Septuagint, often attests a deeper understanding and interpretation of the Scriptures, on the basis of the developed belief of later Judaism. It thus furthers the investigation of the 'fuller sense', so much so that in recent years voices have again been raised to maintain the inspiration of this translation.

Later, the same Old Testament was read by the primitive apostolic Church in the light of the incarnation and the resurrection of Christ from the dead. Finally, we read the same Scriptures in the light of the process of salvation at work in the Church, which is directed by the same Spirit which inspired the Old Testament. It will not do to be as naïve as in medieval times and try to find every truth in Scripture, because it is sustained by the Spirit who is also the inspirer of Scripture. *'Omne verum dictum est sensus Sacrae Scripturae'*, said the medieval scholastics, 'Anything that is said in truth is also the sense of Scripture'! We must first find the Christological or Mariological meaning in a prolongation of the primary literal sense, which is to be established by exegetical methods. Only then can we speak of a 'fuller sense' or of a Christological or Mariological meaning in an Old Testament text.

All this leads to the conclusion that the dogmatic theologian has the continuing task, as once the apostolic Church itself had, of reading Sacred Scripture again and again, retrospectively; and in doing so, to presuppose the findings of Christian exegesis. St Thomas said long ago that 'even the true prophets did not comprehend everything that the Holy Spirit intended in their visions, words and actions' (*S. Th.* II–II, q. 173, a. 4). Only in and through the life of the Church, under the guidance of the teaching office, which exercises its protection under the influence of the Spirit who spoke through the prophets, can the divine quality of the inspired human word become fully evaluated in express consciousness. By the word of Scripture which says, 'Receive ye the Holy Spirit' (Jn 20: 22–23), is meant primarily the gift of the Spirit by which the Scriptures are read in a 'Christian' way. (Compare Jn 16: 13.)

For the dogmatic theologian, the Scripture is not just one more document among the many which he has to investigate. For him too, Scripture has an irreductible, unique and primary significance. No doubt, the faithful receive the word of God from the Church, but what they receive through this channel is none other than the word of God to which the Scripture testifies. Biblical theology and dogmatics cannot be opposed to one another, in spite of the difference in the immediate view-points of each. The Church, Tradition, can only present to us, under the guidance of the Spirit, what Christ himself said, did and was, an Event to which the apostolic message (*kerygma*) gives direct testimony. And this message reaches us directly in the Sacred Scriptures. Just as the post-apostolic Church rests on the apostolic authority, on the sacraments and on the ecclesiastical preaching of the faith, so too does it rest on the Sacred Scriptures, which stand in the form of a missal beside the chalice on the altar. The day is past in which, under the influence of anti-Protestant leanings, the vital significance of Christian Scripture-reading was looked upon askance. And one consequence is that we can see in dogmatic theology in recent years the development of a newer, more authentic character. Just because Scripture is a testimony to the primary origin of the reality which in theology we call 'Tradition', Scripture is really the 'fountain-head of divine tradition'. The Church wins its dogmas not by theological conclusions from Scripture, but by re-discovering its own living dogma in the Scripture. Hence Yves Congar says: 'I respect the science of the exegete, and I ask him continually for information. But I do not recognize his teaching authority' (*Vraie et fausse réforme dans l'Eglise*, 1950).

The last word on revelation is not spoken by the Christian exegete. For revelation, though it comes through the channels of the process of salvation which took place in the Old and New Dispensations, and through the inspired testimony in its regard, is addressed to all men of all ages. What believers, under the guidance of the Holy Spirit who works in the Church, have made their own out of this process may be, as regards express formulation, something different from what Sacred Scripture has made its own of the process of salvation. But the biblical expression remains the expression of the same faith as the Church now confesses. On the level of articulate expression, therefore, there is a growth, a progress, in the course of Church history with regard to Sacred Scripture. In this progress dogmatics plays the role of servant, but this role it neither can nor will abandon, to be replaced entirely by the work of the exegete and biblical theologian.

On the other hand, the exegete has, as we have said above, a critical function to exercise with regard to dogmatics, because the exegete studies the first beginnings, which are guaranteed by God, and the trends to which that beginning gave rise. And these original trends, because they are so thoroughly directed by their beginnings, remain always a critical court of appeal with regard to the further course of the movement then set on foot. It is in this sense that we can make our own the dictum of Karl Rahner concerning Scripture: 'It is the ruling principle of dogmatic theology'.

In the light of this brief exposition we may draw the conclusion that dogmatic theologians often enough take too little or too much from the Scriptures. The simple reason is that they take Scripture only as a source-book for proof-texts in favour of really or ostensibly established dogmatic theses. On the contrary, however, they should start from the Christian faith and strive to follow step by step, and indeed share, the transition from the Old to the New Testament. They should strive to share personally the movement of the early apostolic Church as it sought, by means of themes from the Old Testament, to approach the Christian mystery of salvation in the Incarnation. They should strive to join in this effort of the *'fides quaerens intellectum'*, the faith seeking understanding of itself, of which the New Testament itself gives us so clear an example.

Rudolf
Schnackenburg

THE DOGMATIC EVALUATION
OF THE NEW TESTAMENT

An exegete who has to pronounce upon the dogmatic
evaluation of the New Testament has also to overcome
several hindrances. Some come from himself because, being
an exegete, his main interest is to establish precisely the
original meaning of the text as it was understood by its
author and as it was conditioned by his mentality. Others
come from the fact that he must take account of the reaction of the theologians, who will perhaps raise their eye-
brows at what seems to them a trespass on other men's
fields. However, if he is asked by the dogmatic theologians,
and if in addition he is allowed to consider his discourse
merely as a contribution to a round-table conference, he
will not wish to disregard their invitation. After all, what
binds and obliges us is the fact that in spite of the varying
structures of the disciplines we teach, we are all Catholic
theologians, who perform all their theological work within
the Church and in the framework of its doctrines of faith
and its basic theological principles.

All theological controversies and tensions are therefore

more or less exploratory flights over a country, or perhaps excavations in a country, which is still well known to all of us and which is the common mother country of all: though we may arrive at different points. It is precisely to learn to know it better that we soar to the heights or descend to the depths—and then grow heated about our divergent views and opinions. But none of us wish to leave the firm ground of the Church, or emigrate from our land.

The remarks we make here on the dogmatic evaluation of the New Testament from the stand-point of the exegete are confined to some personal considerations and observations. They do not claim to treat the subject either systematically or exhaustively. Their aim is rather to promote reflexion and discussion. There is, however, one thing which is desirable in discussion between dogmatic theologians and New Testament scholars, and that is that they be prepared to come down to cases, not merely to talk in general about Church and Bible, or about difficulties of interpreting the Bible, but to discuss texts, at least selected texts which can serve as examples. The dogmatic theologian must therefore agree to come down from the heights of speculation and deal with texts, while the exegete must strive to rise to the view-point of the Church's faith and the set of problems posed by dogmatics. The meeting-point will be the actual words of Sacred Scripture. The dogmatic theologian starts from the preaching of the Church, takes it logically further, but returns to the Bible to ask for answers. The exegete investigates the text of Scripture with all the means provided by history and criticism, but does not wish to depart from the mind of the Church as it has been determined by dogma.

The first thing will be to establish that a dogmatic evaluation of Scripture is justifiable even from the viewpoint of the Catholic exegete. No doubt the dogmatic theologian does not need such a permission from the exegete, and he may even reject it indignantly. But since he is always trying to find a basis for the doctrines of the Church and for his own theological opinions in the Scripture, perhaps he will not find it unwelcome to see that his procedures are confirmed in the New Testament by some observations of the exegete. The primitive Church, as the New Testament shows, also used Sacred Scripture to 'give reasons' for its faith. It used the Old Testament, and in a way that might well be called 'dogmatic'. We all know that it contemplated the Old Testament 'Christologically', and used it in that sense. Its faith in Christ was fixed by the self-revelation of Jesus and the event of the resurrection. And for this faith, as a confirmation, it sought and found places in the Old Testament. For it was the conviction of the primitive Church that God had predicted through his prophets the salvific events of the New Testament, and indeed not a few concrete details of the story of Christ, and that God had brought these prophecies to their fulfilment.

This is not, of course, a simple matter of thinking ourselves justified in applying the same method of interpretation as that used by the primitive Church and the New Testament writers. St Paul, for instance, undoubtedly used certain rabbinical methods which went beyond the literal sense and even gave it new turns. He did not even shrink from expanding the actual words or from changing them. Can we do so to-day? Hardly any dogmatic theologian will be courageous enough for that. The fact is that the problem of the use of Scripture in the primitive Church, and the basic principles which are its consequence, have not yet been worked out. There remain many things to be considered. Was not St Paul's procedure the child of its times, and so confined to that time? And do his statements gain their binding force less from such argumentation than from his dignity as an Apostle of Jesus Christ and an inspired writer? Is new knowledge gained by such scriptural proofs, or do they not rather serve as secondary arguments, valid perhaps for those days, in view of truths of faith which are already certain from the New Testament revelation? Or are they perhaps a theological type of knowledge which are indeed valuable, but not necessary to the faith, as for instance when Abraham is claimed as the prototype and father of all believers? Are we bound to hold that Jesus' domicile in Nazareth was foretold by a text of Scripture, 'He will be called a Nazarene'—a text which in any case cannot be verified?

Let us leave such difficulties aside for the moment, however, and consider something fundamental. It was not the procedure of the primitive Church to establish the literal sense of the Old Testament by means of historical and critical research. Certain of its faith through the revelation of Jesus Christ and the preaching of the Apostles, it 'evaluated dogmatically' the Old Testament on the basis of this possession of the faith. When we have prescinded from all that is conditioned by the epoch, and all that is questionable in the procedure, there still remains the fact that the Church did not go from Scripture to faith, but from faith to Scripture. And that may well be the fundamental starting-point of the dogmatic theologian.

But we need not even have recourse to this debatable relationship of the early Church to the Old Testament Scriptures. There appears in the primitive Church itself, as recently acquired knowledge of exegesis shows, a relationship between revelation, tradition and Church preaching which seems to justify a dogmatic approach to the New Testament, as source of revelation. Before the apostolic tradition and the New Testament revelation contained therein were committed to any form of writing, there comes the oral preaching of the Apostles, the ecclesiastical preaching of the faith. And even the written record of the apostolic preaching still shows us that the main thing was not the committal to writing but the right understanding of its contents, not the fixed form of words but the living conviction of the faith. This is particularly clear in the Gospel of St John, where the discourses of Jesus are reported in a new language which has clearly been formed by theology and the actions of Jesus are interpreted in a profounder sense, and yet the certainty of unaltered faithfulness with regard to the revelation abides, because the Paraclete leads unto all truth (Jn 16:13). The author therefore takes, with regard to the words and deeds of Jesus, an attitude as confident and as free as that of the primitive Church toward the Old Testament. He investigates the declarations and discourses of Jesus, not from the point of view of a critical exegete, but from the point of view of his faith in Christ, which he shares with the Church, and which he uses to throw light on the meaning and content of the life of Jesus.

Though the exegete begins with a critical investigation of tradition, he too must be led by the Christian faith of the primitive Church when he moves on to the theological interpretation of the declarations of Jesus. Indeed, he must do more, and keep in mind the developed and assured doctrine of the present day, as it is preserved by the teaching authority of the Church. But his procedures differ in method from those of the dogmatic theologian. He uses the views of the primitive Church as the broad basis from which he throws light on the literal sense of Scripture, while making use of present-day doctrine only as the presupposition, derived from faith, with which he comes to his task of interpretation—a task in which he is otherwise bound by the methods of historical criticism. He has a *sensus fidei*, the mind of a believer. It is this which helps him draw out the deeper theological meaning of the text, preserves him from error, and directs him along particular lines. Thus, it is both a negative and a positive norm. Yet, presupposition must not stand in the way of a strict use of the critical method. On the contrary, these presuppositions must at times be called into question by the text. The dogmatic theologian starts with the doctrine of the Church, and looks back from there to Sacred Scripture, in order to recognize therein the foundations of the faith, and the starting-points of the more highly developed doctrines. Here, of course, he can miss things which are contained in the inexhaustible treasure of Sacred Scripture, and were not later taken up and developed.

Even in New Testament times, theology was not a way of going from the 'bare words' of Jesus to a deeper theological sense. On the contrary, a faith anchored in the Church took over the words of Jesus, disclosed their deeper meaning, cleared up any doubts that arose, and formed the confession of faith. True, this leaves many problems open. Who is entitled to do this? Only the Apostle who is called to be an interpreter of revelation, and the inspired writer? Or any theologian who is part of the orthodox community and accepts the confession of faith? Where are the boundaries to be set to such procedures, and how is certainty to be gained? However these questions are to be answered, our point here is only that such procedures are recognizable in the primitive Church, and that they seem to come close to a dogmatic use of Scripture which stems from the faith of the Church.

Having thus admitted on principle the dogmatic approach and way of thinking, we must now take up some particular problems which are posed by direct contact with the New Testament. Only relatively few texts of Scripture have in fact been claimed by the teaching authority of the Church for a dogmatic decision, and thus had their sense determined. Can the dogmatic theologian, on his own initiative and using his own understanding to survey the teaching of the Church, interpret the New Testament, and perhaps explain texts which seem important to him in a way which goes beyond what the exegete admits as the literal sense, but which seems to be required by the theologian's own dogmatic insight? This question poses many others. Can the dogmatic theologian also appeal to the exegesis of the Fathers of the Church? To the *sensus plenior*, the 'fuller sense'? To doctrinal utterances of the Church which seem to point in the same direction? All these questions, which are still debated among theologians, we must leave aside for now. We are of course agreed that the theologian who wishes to work neatly will begin by confining himself to the literal sense, as worked out by the exegetes. This is the sense which has been designated as authoritative by Pius XII in his encyclical on the Bible, and the theologian will accept it in all questions where he has no assurance for the exegesis by means of a dogmatic doctrine of the Church. All we shall do here is to give some pointers as to how he is to proceed in such questions, and what are his prospects in the matter.

Undoubtedly, the theologian has the right and the duty, according to the principle of his discipline, to take the doctrinal content of a biblical text worked out according to the literal sense, and place it in the whole context of the Catholic faith. He is not confined to biblical theology, but may use the doctrine of the Church as it has been developed in the course of centuries. He will, however, meet with many difficulties. How, for instance, is he going to make St Paul's doctrine of the Church as the body of Christ coincide completely with the doctrine proposed by the Church, which has in the meanwhile been much more richly developed and differentiated, and necessarily expanded by all sorts of problems? In St Paul, many questions are still not explicitly put, such as: Do heretics and schismatics still belong to the body of Christ? What place does Mary occupy in the Church as the body of Christ? How is the relationship between hierarchy and people to be represented in the body of Christ?

The dogmatic theologian will be inclined to find the precise answers already indicated as early as possible in St Paul. He will thereby run the risk of reading meanings into the Pauline texts, and deriving consequences from them which are far from the mind of St Paul. Should he not rather determine which are the decisive truths which the Apostle had at heart, and then explain how the later theology of the Church, down to the present day, is a legitimate continuation and unfolding of St Paul's principles? Or must Sacred Scripture be made to bear the weight of all proofs, including those of the most difficult questions?

We can perhaps take a comparison from another field. Biology has long since recognized that it is wrong to look for the individual elements of the developed organism in the seed or the embryo. And yet the dispositions, the potentiality, and the finality which tend to the organic

whole are already present in the germ. Something anal-
ogous is true also of the 'proof from Scripture'. It is often
quite enough to point out the starting-point or the germ,
from which the later doctrine has then developed. But we
must be careful not to extend this comparison or imagery
from biology to the whole relationship between the Bible
and our present-day doctrine. Apart from the question of
whether all (not authoritatively defined) theological views
are really legitimate developments, we must take into
account the fact that, in the Bible, weighty theological
interests are neglected, many orientations are not developed, certain thoughts are in an impoverished state. Sacred
Scripture, or biblical theology is, in comparison with the
doctrines proposed by dogmatic theology, 'poorer' in many
instances where its utterances have since been deepened
and clarified. On the other hand, it is 'richer' since it has
not yet been so fully exploited, and since it is in fact an
inexhaustible treasure.

There are many questions to which the Bible provides
us with no definite answer, and yet we may call the answers
gained from tradition, from the pronouncements of the
teaching authority, and from sound speculation, really
biblical, in so far as they are in the line of an organic
development. In this effort to find a biblical foundation,
there is, it appears, a particular danger. Some are inclined
to make the biblical imagery an absolute rule, and to use
a sketch, which was there only to make vivid certain
thoughts, as though it were the complete model, from which
further instances might be derived. To take a rather crude
example, is it reasonable and possible to compare Mary
with a particular organ of the body of Christ? In the very
text in which St Paul speaks of various parts of the body
(1 Cor 12) we have only a comparison with an organism,

while the thought of the Body of Christ certainly contains more than does any picture.

It is different in the epistles to the Colossians and the Ephesians, where Christ is the head, and the Church his body. There the relationship between Christ and Church must be explained in terms of the image of 'body' which is there proposed. Dogmatic theology has hitherto perhaps performed this task insufficiently. The very close connexion between the 'Body of Christ' which bled to death on the Cross and the 'ecclesiastical' Body of Christ built up by the Spirit has, as far as I know, hardly been considered by theologians, much less sufficiently clarified. They are perhaps hindered by the other concepts and categories which they use. The content of each piece of imagery must be carefully analysed. Often enough, if we renounce an exegesis which clings too closely to the metaphor, we shall even be spared difficulties. It would be incorrect to try to contest the idea of Law Court in the Pauline 'justification'. But it is in fact just a metaphor from the field of jurisprudence, to which are adjoined other means of expression which come closer to the heart of the matter and confirm, not the doctrine of an 'imputed' justice, but a real, essential sanctification.

So the dogmatic theologian must also take pains to understand the biblical way of speaking and thinking, and he may not be false to them. That sounds perhaps disheartening. But it gives rise to very positive tasks, for the theologian and for the exegete. The art of the exegete consists in taking thoughts which are clothed in a certain language and grasping them clearly, pressing on to the kernel and rendering them clearly for the present day. The dogmatic theologian seems to be called to wider fields of endeavour, because he has to keep in view centuries of theological development, formation of concepts and doctrinal progress. Many influences were at work, chiefly the adoption of Greek philosophy, to transfer biblical thought into other categories. We need only think of Christology. In the New Testament period, it is still entirely depicted in terms of the process of salvation, but after that it is more and more absorbed by the Two-Natures doctrine and the theology of the Incarnation. Or if we think of sanctifying grace, we find a doctrine which corresponds to the biblical terms of 'spirit' and 'life'. Should not the dogmatic theologian succeed in describing this transition from one set of categories to another, and at the same time demonstrate the continuity and legitimacy of such a development and give us a better understanding of it? Perhaps he must be daring enough even to undertake a new 'translation' for the benefit of modern man and to satisfy the needs of to-day's preaching. This is in fact being done in many promising essays. The New Testament certainly gives him the right to do this, since we can clearly see the efforts made by the great theologians of the New Testament, St Paul, St John and the author of the Epistle to the Hebrews to bring their own way of thinking and representing things into line with the attitudes and experiences of their hearers or readers, on various levels of philosophy and environment.

If one keeps the different categories of thought in mind, many difficulties that arise between exegete and theologian may be cleared away. Let us see at least one example of this. For the embarrassing saying of Jesus, 'The Father is greater than I' (Jn 14 : 28), the dogmatic theologian readily uses the solution offered by St Cyril of Alexandria, St John Chrysostom and St Augustine, that Jesus according to his human nature is under the Father. But that does not fit the context. The difficulty is only solved by thinking in terms of the process of salvation. The Father, whom Jesus in his earthly life reveres as the greater, will now show himself the greater with regard to Jesus too, by glorifying him. And the disciples ought to rejoice at this, because the glorified Lord will be all the better able to apply his love and his power to save. It would be the task of dogmatic theology to show how the Johannine theology, which testifies equally to the unity of the Son and the Father and to the subordination of the Son to the Father, is none other than the classic Christology formulated at Chalcedon, in spite of its different point of view.

There must be many points at which New Testament theology can be attached to modern man's way of thinking and understanding reality, and they can be fruitfully taken up and developed by the combined work of exegesis and theology. The dynamic way of thinking in the Bible, which regards history chiefly in its significance, is certainly welcome to the 'existential' thinking of to-day. Every man, including the Christian, is seen in his historical state and situation, and is shown the way in which he can escape from his experience of being lost and cast aside. To-day the chief consideration is the way in which man is menaced and shattered in his very existence as man. But our faith gives us many pointers to a true image of man: likeness to God, redemption, sonship with God, Jesus as our brother, Mary as the pure maiden glorified in her body, and so on.

It seems, however, that we find nowhere a vision as unified and attractive as in St Paul: Christ the new Adam, the progenitor of redeemed humanity, to whom we are united and incorporated, a new creation in him already, a new man according to the image of his Creator, and yet still called to 'put on' by moral effort the new man, in order to attain finally to the full form of redeemed man. This full form is Christ, the risen Lord, the conqueror of the powers of destruction, conqueror finally of all-destructive death. He is 'the first-born among many brothers', to whom we are already joined in order one day to be completely like to him, when we shall be clad in the form of his glory, just as we bore the image of the earthly Adam (Rom 8:29; 1 Cor 15:49; Phil 3:21). We can also place Mary, especially since the definition of the Assumption, in this field of vision, since she, the first of creatures, attained this perfect form by the grace of God and shines before us now in a pure humanity, gloriously transformed. There still remains the vocabulary to be used in preaching, if we are to share with our fellow-men of to-day these deep and fruitful thoughts.

This already means that the dogmatic theologian, when dealing with the New Testament, is by no means bound to deny himself speculative thought. Let us take for instance man's likeness to God. What the Bible says about this will appear meagre to the dogmatic theologian, though not unfruitful under objective theological interpretation. But he is free to clothe this important thought with more flesh from the theology of the Fathers, from scholastic speculation, and his own competence. Likewise every reasonable exegete will be content when the dogmatic theologian takes the trinitarian expressions of the New Testament and, following the dogmatic explanations of the succeeding centuries, gives a profounder insight into their meaning and develops them more richly—provided that this is not done by jumping to conclusions.

For instance, the point of view of the exegete does not allow us to refer the Johannine sayings about the Son's

proceeding from the Father to the inner-trinitarian processes without further ado. St John has always in mind
the mission of the Son in the world, the descent of the Son
of Man from heaven. But the mission of the Son *ad extra*
does indeed take up, in a new and special way, the relationship which is verified within the Holy Trinity by the
eternal procession of the Son from the Father. And so it
implies, when one takes into account also the statements
about the essential relation of the Incarnate Son to the
Father, the dogma of the Trinity. The same is true of
statements about the Spirit, or as the case may be, the
Paraclete. The dogmatic theologian is fully justified in
explaining them by the personal character of the Holy
Spirit and his relationship to the Father and the Son. Even
though the Spirit in St Paul stands firstly for the life of the
risen Christ which flows over into those who are united
to Christ, that is, from the point of view of dogma, for the
gratia capitis, the grace of the Head, this does not exclude
the indwelling of the Holy Spirit in the soul of the man
in the state of grace. Of course the question of how St Paul
understood the metaphors of the Temple and the Indwelling of the Holy Spirit is still there. But the dogmatic
theologian, in view of later theological developments and
Church teaching, has certainly the right to give an answer
in the fullest sense of the doctrine of grace and the Trinity.

Finally, an example from another field. The exegete,
using his own methods, will hardly be able to establish
perfectly from New Testament texts the sacrificial character of the Eucharist. But the dogmatic theologian, while
recognizing the boundaries set to his knowledge by the
New Testament itself has, according to the principles of
his discipline, the possibility of throwing light on this
sacrificial character and determining it more closely. Once

more, this should not be undertaken in a way the exegete could contest, as for instance by a reference to the breaking of bread by Jesus, since this indicates no 'breaking of the legs' or sacrificial death, but was rather the prelude to the distribution of the bread among the participants, and is thus a gesture which founds a community. But the cultic and sacramental representation of the sacrificial death offers even a New Testament starting-point for the sacrificial character of the Eucharistic rite. All these examples are on the lines indicated: we are not to take too much from a text or to twist its sense. But the dogmatic theologian can show how much more fruitful a text becomes when viewed in the whole context of the Catholic faith, and how much more deeply it has been drawn upon by tradition and the development of doctrine than is possible to the exegete when exploring the literal sense.

After this obeisance to dogmatic theology, the exegete may now call attention to certain *limits of speculation*, which are set by the New Testament. A system inserted into the whole cosmos of the faith may well seek for support in the text of the New Testament, even if only looking for a germ therein. But the theologian may not do so by ignoring the literal sense, or by going against it. At most, he may transcend it, and thus the sense he decides upon must be such that it does not exclude the speculative possibilities in question. Here exegesis must be critic and judge, and the theologian may well be obliged to accept such criticism of his urge to speculation. For instance, it would be a doubtful and dangerous procedure to try to give precisions about the nature of the risen body based on the fact that the Risen Lord, according to St Luke, ate something in the presence of his disciples. The exegete finds the inten-

11

tion of the narrative perfectly clear. It is to testify to the reality of the resurrection of Jesus, and the reality of his body. It does not intend to give details about the nature of that body.

In addition, we know that Jesus himself stressed the completely different nature of the resurrection when he said, 'They are like the angels in heaven' (Mk 12:25). Once again, it would be risky to attach any speculation to the 'angelic nature' of the Risen Lord, since this saying—which merely makes a comparison, as the particle 'like' shows (though Luke 20:36 has 'of angelic nature')—was uttered only from a special viewpoint: 'They shall neither marry nor be given in marriage'. Such ways of putting a theological truth are often of wide importance. As is well known, the thought of the 'angelic nature' among the Fathers and long after them had a marked influence, which was not always healthy, on the motivation of virginity. The basic rule is that a saying must not be taken out of its context and detached from the intention of the speaker or writer, which must be always observed in such matters. Finally, St Paul (1 Cor 15:36-44) propounds with all desirable clarity how the glorified body differs from all earthly bodies, and what are its particularities. But even the Apostle can be misunderstood, as if he were speaking merely of a 'flesh' visible to eyes and with a splendour like the brightness of the stars. Even these are only analogies, which hardly intend to impart a definite view of the nature of the risen body.

This does not mean that we cannot make certain positive statements about the risen body, such as that it is immortal, that in the just it is glorified, penetrated by God's Spirit and power. But we must do justice to the fact that, as long as we are bound to our earthly bodies, we can have no concrete images of the risen body, and indeed of life in general in the world to come. The rather marked difference between the Vulgate Latin text and the original Greek of 1 Corinthians 15:51 is hard to pass judgment on. The original says: 'We shall not all die, but we shall all be changed'. The Vulgate says: 'All will indeed arise, but not all will be changed'. The Vulgate clearly has in mind the general resurrection, and means in the second phrase that not all—namely the damned—shall be exalted to divine glory. According to the original text, St Paul is thinking only of those who are united to Christ and, in contrast to other Jewish views, proclaims it as a mystery, that at the resurrection a change will take place in the living as well as in the dead. They will all have a body of a completely different quality, and that immediately, not only gradually. This is in opposition to such Jewish writings as the Apocalypse of Baruch (in Syriac). May we now speculate further about the bodies of the damned, on the basis of the Vulgate text? Such a question must, one supposes, be decided by the dogmatic theologians themselves. However, there are enough cases where the New Testament, by its negative delimitation, or its deliberately reserved statements, counsels against further dogmatic speculation. Such would be the question of predestination, the number of the elect (see Lk 13:23 f), the virginity of Mary *in partu*, at child-bearing, (see Lk 1:35 ff; Mt 1:20–23), and perhaps also the psychological processes of Jesus, to name but a few.

But there are cases where the text can provide *difficulties* to which the dogmatic theologian must be prepared to give answers according to the presuppositions of his own discipline. Here above all we must recall the sayings about the *'kenosis'* (the 'self-emptying'), the 'Ignorance', and the sufferings of Christ. In these matters the exegete can offer only limited help. He can indeed help to explain what is meant by the 'self-emptying' of Christ in Philippians 2:7, somewhat on the lines of a voluntary renunciation of the divine glory, the transition from the state of divine being to that of human lowliness. P. Henry, in the *Supplément au Dictionnaire de la Bible* (V. 7–161), speaks of *'condition divine'* and *'état kénotique'* (divine condition and kenotic state). But how precisely that is compatible with the hypostatic union, and how far the emptying-out makes itself effective in the earthly state of Christ—these are difficult questions, which the dogmatic theologian will have to explain as far as possible in terms of speculation. The testimony of the Gospels can help him on only to a limited extent. To be sure, what they narrate about the behaviour of Jesus, and even about his emotional feelings, is considerable. But they give us little insight into the interior life of Jesus. And since they are written to give a narrative which is really the proclamation of his salvific coming, speaking, and acting, they hardly intend to describe the movements of his soul. Hence they transmit to us the saying: 'That day and that hour no man knows, and not even the angels in heaven, nor the Son, but only the Father' (Mk 13:32)—without any Christological commentary.

The exegete will take great care to see that clear New Testament sayings are not emptied of their significance, levelled off or rendered harmless, even though he can understand that the dogmatic theologian would not like to have anybody call into question the results he has won by deduction from dogma. But as in the question of inspiration, there must be found a process of dialectical *rapprochement*, as it were, from both sides. The problem of inspiration cannot be settled one-sidedly by dogmatic postulates, nor again by the mere registration of the empirical facts of the Bible.

The same is true of other special problems, such as that of Christology. Many exegetes are inclined to extend the notion of 'self-emptying' so far that in practice they see only the man Jesus speaking in many of his sayings. Also, they often recognize him only as man in his actions and in his passion. They see his divinity only as it were at high points of revelation, in some special words of self-revelation and in some 'epiphany narratives', where the divinity has a momentary manifestation. This is certainly too one-sided, and its insufficiency can be seen at once in the way which the Gospel of St John presents Jesus, where he is put before us, from beginning to end, in a divine glory which is concealed and yet discloses itself to the faith. On the other hand, the dogmatic theologian seems to be in danger of not doing justice to hard and uncomfortable New Testament texts because he is concerned for the dogma of the hypostatic union and its inescapable consequences, such as the beatific vision in the human nature of Jesus. To take a relatively easy example: It says in Mark 6:5 that Jesus could perform no miracles in Nazareth. To solve this problem by saying that he could not because he would not is too easy a way out. It is not in the text, and it is not hinted at in any way. The difficult 'He could not' must be left to stand as it is—though the text has already been given a milder version in St Matthew's gospel—and explained as it stands. The answer should be on the lines of saying that Jesus was bound by the mandate of his heavenly Father to work no miracles where crude unbelief confronted him. He was therefore in fact incapable of doing miracles there, by the divine disposition. The dogmatic theologian would have to ask further what consequences this limitation of Christ's power, this 'emptying out' has for Christology, and more precisely for Christ's obedience.

These, however, are only examples for what are surely many grave questions of interpretation. It is not only the exegete who must not make things too easy for himself by starting with a conception of the 'emptying-out', the kenosis, of which the dogmatic theologian, not unjustly, is suspicious. The theologian too must take real pains to look for solutions, as in the question of inspiration, which do not give the impression of emasculating the concrete sayings of the New Testament. This brings before us a set of problems which is the distinguishing feature of the relationship between dogmatic and historical theology. They are problems which seem to call for a constant struggle, an unending dialogue between both disciplines, both of which have been called into existence by the historical nature of revelation. And though they are often engaged in a painful effort to disengage themselves from each other, they are still intrinsically related to each other, as the two main branches of our theology.

We are therefore directed to a dialectical conversation with each other, a debate that is full of tensions, that moves to the centre of truth after starting as it were from two different points which are poles apart. But we are also directed to a common labour at questions which are common to us both, the still unmastered tasks of a modern theology, which cannot be answered at all except by co-operation. Let us recall the question of eschatology, of 'the last days', and the problem of 'de-mythizing' connected with it—which has by no means been totally solved. Perhaps after all we should make an effort to give a properly

worked out and Catholic interpretation along existentialist lines. We can see at once what the problem is by
envisaging two New Testament phenomena, which we
cannot vaporize away by apologetic efforts. These are the
expectation of the imminent end, and the promises of a
future described in apocalyptic categories which sound
mythological in the extreme. We can still succeed, relatively easily, in detaching from the real revelation the
sayings about the spatial universe, which was then looked
on as geocentric and, more precisely, as consisting of three
storeys. The ascension of Christ and his descent to hell are
to be considered here.

But things are not so simple with regard to future
expectations. The expectation of the imminent coming of
the full kingdom of God in the preaching of Jesus, and
likewise the expectation of the imminent coming of Christ
in the primitive Church, to which many New Testament
texts testify, are facts we cannot deny. Rather, we must
master them theologically and explain them without any
loss of dogmatic truths. We cannot concede that Jesus
committed an error with regard to the end, no matter how
unimportant we say such an error may have been; nor can
we maintain that the primitive Church or individual New
Testament, that is to say, inspired writers, suffered from
an illusion. We have certainly no need to speak of a delay
in the Second Coming, because it would be very difficult
to prove that Jesus gave any definite date, or that the
primitive Church held to the imminent Coming of Christ
as a doctrine of faith. But there was an expectation of an
imminent end, and it calls for a positive attitude on the
part of theologians. All the more so, since the expectation
of the end, on the part of Jesus and the primitive Church,
can hardly be dismissed as merely something conditioned

by its times, and hence theologically negligible. It clearly has relevance for all expectations of the end, and therefore matters to us Christians of to-day also.

With regard to Jesus' expectation of the end, the exegete might well ask the theologian if and how far one can attribute to Jesus a prophetic attitude, by virtue of which— in spite of all his superiority on other grounds to the Old Testament prophets, in his quality of bringer of the absolute revelation and the eschatological salvation—he was limited to the prophetic manner of seeing and speaking, that is, to making the word of God 'topical' for his contemporaries, and to a perspective of time which may be called 'telescoped'. As regards the expectation of the end in the writers of the New Testament, we must ask whether we can distinguish between their personal opinions or hopes, and their authentic teaching of revelation, which remains authoritative.

It would appear that the Biblical Commission, in Answer XIV of June 18, 1915, has already answered in the negative to the question 'whether the Apostles, although they teach no error, being under the inspiration of the Holy Spirit, still express their own human opinions, in which they can err or be deceived' (*Enchiridion Biblicum*[2], No. 419). But it must be observed that here the emphasis is on 'error or deception'. A personal hope, which has not taken on the character of irrefragable certainty, does not appear to be thereby excluded. B. Rigaux (*Les Epîtres aux Thessaloniciens*, Paris, 1956, p. 226) rejects therefore, and rightly so, the expression 'illusion' and prefers to speak, with F. Prat and other Catholic exegetes, of their 'hopes'. It would be indeed the duty of the dogmatic theologian to give the precise meaning and bearing of that decision of the Biblical

Commission, and explain to the exegetes what opinions are dogmatically defensible in this difficult question.

The problems posed here do not seem to have been sufficiently considered by the dogmatic theologians as yet. Hitherto, perhaps, an exegesis dominated by apologetics has given the impression that the texts which speak of an imminent end could be interpreted as though there were no really imminent expectation of the end in terms of time. What then if one is convinced, like B. Rigaux in his extensive commentary on the Epistles to the Thessalonians, or like F. Tillmann in his earlier (1909) work on the Second Coming of Christ according to the Epistles of St Paul, that St Paul seriously awaited the Second Coming in his own lifetime, as his earlier epistles show? Even after St Paul, the expectation of the near end did not die out in the primitive Church, as the testimony of the Revelation of St John is enough to prove.

Here, then, theological considerations must begin, to strive on the one hand to clear the inspired writers of the New Testament from the suspicion of error, and on the other to take up positively their essential interest, which was to maintain a constant expectation of the end in such a way that it coloured all Christian existence, and render it fruitful for present-day preaching. This last leads necessarily to a sort of 'existential interpretation'. Bultmann and his followers use this to cut away all future eschatology, to re-interpret it as the eschatological self-understanding of the Christian in the present, which finally leaves us only with a believer's 'open-mindedness' for the future. This will not do. We need an interpretation which will exhibit the future events in their transcendent essence, and in their character of existentially present challenge.

Thus the problem of time becomes pressing once more,

with regard to the New Testament order of salvation, which is bound up with time but determined by the eternal, supratemporal action of God. Yet the eschatological problem becomes even vaster if we look at the final events themselves, as described in 'apocalyptic' terms. We are thankful to Karl Rahner for his essay on the theological principles to be used in explaining eschatological sayings, which appeared in the *Zeitschrift für Katholische Theologie*, 1960. These principles are prudent and well balanced. The difficulty arises only with their application to the actual sayings of the New Testament.

What parts of them can be considered as 'expendable', mere 'apocalyptic furniture' described in virtue of the apocalyptic views of the day? And what is the authoritative revelation which is embedded therein? We all agree that the sound of the last trumpet (1 Cor 15:52) and the voice of the Archangel (1 Thes 4:16) only stand for the hour of God, which will then have struck. The 'first' and 'then' of 1 Thessalonians 4:16 ('*first* will those who have died in Christ arise, *then* shall we, the living, those who remain, be brought to meet Christ along with them'), are easily reduced to one moment, in view of 1 Corinthians 15:52. Likewise, the clouds on which the Son of Man comes, according to Mark 13:26, like those on which we are carried, according to 1 Thessalonians 4:17, to meet Christ in the air, can also be easily understood as conventional requisites in the description of apocalyptic scenes. But what of the gathering of the elect by the angels of God from all quarters of the heavens, of which the so-called Synoptic Apocalypse speaks, (Mt 24; Mk 13; Lk 21)? How does this compare with the meeting with Christ in 1 Thessalonians 4? Are there not two different theological thoughts here, and have they not been given two very different expressions, even in their imagery? Place and time, as described in the final events, show such strong divergence in various New Testament texts, that when all are taken together, one must take them as a necessarily incompetent expression of the truth that the age to come and the final new creation have arrived, which are incomprehensible to us as long as our minds are tied to this age, and the hitherto existing world.

The same is also true, to a certain degree, of the New Testament accounts of the appearances of the Risen Lord. Our thinking, which is bound to the dimensions of time and space and which must always have an imaginative accompaniment, is here no longer adequate. We can still indeed *distinguish* between the return of Christ, the resurrection of the dead, the judgment and the new creation of all things. But we cannot *describe* them, or fix their sequence. In other words we are here forced in great part to separate the theological and revelational assertions from the images, the children of their times, in which they are embodied. It is the same task as is done on the account of creation in Genesis, namely to distinguish between the revealed content and the literary forms in which it is clothed, that is, the language of its day and the imagery in which it is presented. The task has yet to be done for New Testament eschatology. How far can and must we go in this matter? That is a question which must occupy exegetes and dogmatic theologians in common.

All the remarks which we have made here were rather aimed at indicating and illustrating the problems than at really dealing with them. But they should make us somewhat more circumspect in our treatment of the New Testament as a document of revelation. In any case, one thing should be clear. Both sides, the exegetes and the theologians, must bring understanding to bear on each other's problems. They must understand that in the end these are problems which are posed to both of us in common, in order to remove difficulties of faith and philosophy from the path of modern man and to disclose to him more clearly and profoundly 'the inexhaustible riches of Christ' (Eph 3 : 8).

Heinrich
Gross

TRANSPOSITION OF THEMES AS PRINCIPLE OF FORM AND TRADITION IN THE OLD TESTAMENT

One of the concerns of the theology of the Old Testament is that exegesis should not lose itself in details or commit its findings to separate compartments, but that it should bring all its explanations into a general picture, where they all can be heard and given their true value. Anyone who surveys the results of Old Testament exegesis will recognize that certain assertions of different texts are closely connected in substance, that they stand in an organic structure which points on to a set end; indeed, that many of them represent sign-posts along equally central lines in the progress of the event of revelation. Another astonishing observation shows further that often the same assertions are used for different levels of revelation and are adopted for several biblical texts. But not all of these can be understood on the same level. These motifs or themes appear rather as *transposed*. As each new height is reached in God's intervention in revelation, they receive in consequence a new meaning and demand a new understanding.

In this process of taking up and developing certain given modes of expression, the similarity in the usage of these motifs points to a certain continuity and deliberate purpose in the central lines of revelation, from the first utterance on. This 'transposing of motifs', as this formative principle of Old Testament tradition may be called, gives then an insight into the inner process of growth in revelation. It means therefore that the sacred writers, each in turn often starting where his forerunner had stopped, not merely take up given themes, but endow them with a deeper content and so transform them. They adapt the fulness of their content to their own days, by bringing out their own specific mission and duty. Using categories of assertions which have been evolved and enriched in content, they lend the new stage of revelation its proper expression. At the same time it is quite possible that these modes of expression live on in other parts of the Old Testament, on the level first reached and expressed, but in changed historical situations. This principle which is at work in the Bible for the development of literary forms and the transmission of tradition, 'the transposing of motifs', we shall now propound with regard to the theologically relevant ideas of Wandering, Sion, Peace, and above all, Covenant. These may at first give the impression of having been chosen arbitrarily. But the principle of transposition brings them together on the level of the eschatological assertion. Our method does not here allow us, of course, to offer a detailed exegesis for particular items. But decisive items will be treated, and in horizontal sections, as it were, their transposition will be noted throughout the Old Testament.

According to Genesis 12: 1 Abraham is thus summoned by

God: 'Leave thy homeland and thy kinsmen and thy father's house, and go into the land which I shall show thee'. It is the common opinion of all commentators that this verse reveals a new departure in the divine act of salvation. God makes a new beginning with his work of setting up his kingship, the salvation of men. To fulfil his purpose, he calls Abraham out of his national, tribal and family ties, and places him as a pilgrim in closer proximity to himself. In the obedience to God's call, in the wandering which God has commanded, God's plan begins to be fulfilled. It does not merely separate Abraham from the community of peoples, it also gives him a special place, and is the base of a new way of existing before God. For when God commands Abraham to become a wanderer, it is not just to reach a goal within this world, no matter how much earthly promises appear in the foreground. The call is to a task beyond this world, which finds clear expression in the context of our verse, the promise of blessing in Genesis 12:2 f. If at every beginning something essential and determinative occurs, then this summons from God to Abraham has an exceptional importance, as results in fact from the progress of the revelation.

Indeed, in many ways the way in which God led his chosen people through Moses gives the impression of being a parallel to the destiny of Abraham. Among the similarities are above all the exodus from Egypt, the march through the desert and the wandering before reaching the promised land, whither God, as once he called Abraham, now summons the whole people of Israel. This purpose is first made known when Moses is called by the words recorded in Exodus 3:8: 'Therefore have I come down, to save them from the might of the Egyptians and to lead them out of that land into a land flowing with milk and honey'. (This promise goes through the whole Pentateuch like a red thread and is constantly put before the people, to remind it persistently of the unique grace granted them by Yahweh, or to bring out by contrast the gravity of their guilt. See Ex 13:5; 33:2; Lev 20:24; Num 13:27; 14:8; 16:13 f; Deut 6:3; 11:9; 26:9; 27:3; 31:20 f; Jos 5:6.) As in the case of Abraham, but now on a higher level of God's guidance, which reaches the whole people, there stands behind God's summons, as the goal of their wandering, a special covenant to be enacted. (What is said here, by way of exposition and result, coincides from time to time with A. Gros, 'Le Thème de la route dans la Bible', in *Etudes Religieuses*, Brussels-Paris, 1957.) In the covenant given on Sinai, in the solemn foundation of the Old Testament religion, God brings the promise to the Patriarch Abraham to a provisional fulfilment, which is the truly historical goal of the Old Testament.

And finally, when the people has become sedentary, the obligation is laid upon it to go on pilgrimage to Jerusalem three times a year, to appear before Yahweh (Ex 23:17; 34:23). This obligation comes from the intention of making the new relationship to God, constituted by the covenant on Sinai, and the new level of fellowship with him therein achieved, a permanent thing by means of constantly renewed pilgrimage. Only by constantly 'travelling' towards God can this fellowship of the chosen people with God grow and flourish, according to the conceptions of the Old Testament.

This obligation also lays bare a root principle of the divine plan of salvation. Here on earth our fellowship with God can never be a full, comprehensive thing. It is a way of possessing him which must be kept alive in new efforts to meet him, and so deepened and intensified. In other words, man here on earth is always a pilgrim on his way to God.

This theme of pilgrimage receives quite a new intensity, on the highest level of Old Testament revelation, in the eschatological pilgrimage of the peoples described in Is 2:2 f; Mich 4:1 f; Is 60:3-9. 'All the nations shall flow to [Sion], and many peoples shall come and say: "Come, let us go up to the mountain of the Lord, to the house of the God of Jacob".' This is a new, transformed world. The content of the prophetic preaching has been transferred into the 'last days', 'eschatologized', and Sion, the place of God's presence, is also decked out with idealized traits. Now the whole world is visibly under the spell of this lofty mountain and within its field of force. All nations, spontaneously and from a free inner urge, march up this mountain in an eschatological pilgrimage to Yahweh, to share the fulness of salvation granted in the final glory. According to Isaias 25:6-8, the glory is imparted to all the nations in the form of a choice feast, which brings about the closest fellowship with God.

What remains constant, on the first level of the salvation set before Abraham in the distant future, as on the highest level of salvation accomplished in Isaias, is that men must become pilgrims drawing ever closer to God, and that this is the presupposition of salvation. The 'wandering' abides, but it does not stay the same thing; what it involves changes according to the level reached by revelation, which expressed the theme employed in ever-varying modalities. The theme is not just taken over but, as the new content shows clearly, it is 'transposed'. Theologically important in this process is that in marching towards a goal which surpasses the richness of the starting-point, we have a revelation of the way and manner in which, according to the Old Testament, Gods' plan for man's salvation is realized and his kingship enforced at each succeeding stage of revelation. Like the goal itself, its correlative, the motif of pilgrimage, goes through the same gradual process of evolution, as it unfolds itself within the Old Testament revelation.

Soon after David had conquered Sion and made it the capital of his kingdom, which embraced the whole union of the Twelve Tribes of Israel, he had the Ark of the Covenant transferred to Sion (2 Sam 6: 1 f). The special solemnity of the act was dictated not just by political calculations of its purpose and value. We can well ascribe to David 'political calculations' but we must be aware that this was the thinking of a believer who was sincerely a theocratic ruler. The solemn procession in which the ark was brought to its place (2 Sam 6: 1 f), David's sacrifice and cultic dance (2 Sam 6: 13), the offering of peace sacrifices and burnt sacrifices after the ark was installed (6: 18), the special sacrificial banquet, with which we must compare 1 Chronicles 13; 15; 16, show clearly that Yahweh himself, in whose service David acts, has chosen Sion as his dwelling-place in the midst of his people.

In fact, from now on Sion, with the tabernacle and later with the Temple, will be one of the crystallization-points for the further development of belief in Yahweh. More than the geographical situation, it is the value of the ideal attached to Sion which places it ever more firmly in the centre of the Israelite faith. With the Israelite kingdom at the height of its power, a theopolitical entity, Solomon dedicates the Temple and gives the significance of the new dwelling-place of God on Sion its fitting expression. 'That all the peoples of the earth may know that Yahweh is God, and there is no other' (3 Kg 8 : 60). Here the longing for the universality of faith in Yahweh comes to the fore. This universality is to start from Sion and there find its centre of gravity. It is guaranteed and upheld by the permanent residence of Yahweh in his 'Royal Palace' on the mountain of God.

From the beginning, the election of Sion is closely bound up with the election of the Davidic dynasty, which is to be the source and matrix of the messianic expectation in Israel. The two central dominant ideas of 2 Samuel 6 f, the choice of the Davidic dynasty and of Sion by Yahweh, are fitted out from the start with a pregnant theology which almost necessarily calls for a 'transposing' understanding of it in prophecy. In close connexion with its historical significance, the motif of 'Sion as the place of the presence of God' is strongly developed in the equally universal promise of the last days in Isaias 2 : 2-4 (Mich 4 : 1-4), and raised to a new, indeed the highest level, of Old Testament revelation. With this, the historical election of Sion is taken up into eschatology and thereby confirmed. For now the whole world is within the sphere of action of the holy mountain of God (see Is 11 : 9), which has been transformed and stands at the summit of all the mountains. It radiates over the whole world.

The historical Sion is in fact the point on which the eschatological prophecies are centred. This follows, for instance, from the promise of the New Testament in Jeremias. The expressions of Isaias 2 : 3a occur once more in similar words in Jeremias 31 : 6b. In addition, the summons, 'Come, let us go up to the mountain of the Lord', will be obeyed in the future, according to Jeremias 31 : 12, which says, 'They shall come and rejoice on the height of Sion, they shall be jubilant about the salvation of Yahweh'. It has therefore taken over not merely content and style, but even similar wording. Yet before this shining prophecy of the End can become reality, later prophecy has to reckon with the change of situation brought about by the Exile, and so describe a preliminary return of Yahweh to Sion, which is the permanent centre of the post-exilic community's faith too. There Yahweh takes over anew his kingship (Is 57: 7-10; Zach 2: 14 f).

In the course of this development in the history of revelation (from 2 Sam 6 to Is 2: 2-4 into which must be inserted, for its content, Is 52: 7-10) *Sion itself undergoes a change*. From being the relatively unimportant centre of the kingdom of David, it becomes the spiritual centre of Yahweh's universal kingdom. It is well to mark how much of this growing importance of Sion has left traces in the Psalter. In Psalms 76: 3; 78: 68; 132: 13 f, the historical election of Sion by Yahweh is taken up in terms of 2 Samuel 6. In Psalm 50: 2 its beauty is celebrated. In Psalm 46, God's presence there is seen as the basis of impregnable security. In Psalm 48: 2 f, the force of the religion of Yahweh transforms the mythical motif of the Mountain of the Gods in the extreme north, and gives it a poetical turn in terms of Old Testament faith. Psalm 87 presents in a poetic form the outstanding promise of Isaias 2: 2-4 of the eschatological final kingdom of peace, another sign of its significance for the faith of Israel. The transformation of Sion, which increases its importance and validity, follows a process which allows it, at every level of revelation, to do justice to the claims made upon it by its position as the starting-point for the ever more intense and lofty salvation realized by the promised Kingdom.

A third theme, which may be followed up here as an example, demonstrates perhaps even more impressively how an idea can be transformed in the course of the transposing of a motif. We meet the idea of peace in the Old Testament in 3 Kings 5:5, an account of an era of peace which was realized in a period of history: 'Judah and Israel dwelt in security, each man under his vine and his fig-tree, from Dan to Beersheba, all the days of Solomon'. After settling down in the land of Canaan, after the rule of David which had been brimful of wars, as had been the time of his predecessor Saul, the people undoubtedly found it a long-desired benefit that they could experience so many years of peaceful times in the great kingdom of Solomon. One can still feel, in 3 Kings 5:5, the echo of this pleasant contrast to the earlier years of stress and strain. Hence we can understand how the idyll of peace which here gleams forth can afterwards become proverbial, and how these happy years in the united kingdom could live on in the memory of the people even through the Exile, and give rise, time after time, to the ideal of a peace attainable upon earth and passionately longed for. In contrast to the exuberant eschatological promises of the prophets, it is of course a very modest prosperity. For this epoch of peace was confined to the times and the empire of Solomon.

The motif is simply taken over, when the envoys of Sennacherib (4 Kg 18:31) make use of its essential elements in their message to the Jews, to urge them to make peace with the king of Assyria. One will hardly estimate differently the mention of the time of peace under the Maccabee Simon (1 Macc 14:4-15) in the centre of which stands the questionable mention of peace from 3 Kings 5:5. With poetic exuberance, these verses celebrate indeed the prosperous era of Simon's rule. But the peace here thought of, after the previous years of struggle, must no doubt be no more than that of 3 Kings 5:5.

In contrast to this simple repetition of the motif, we find it used again in a different connexion in Micheas 4:4. Its framework is in itself enough to distinguish it from previous occurrences. It is placed in a promise with regard to the End of Days, which is put in the mouth of Yahweh himself. So it appears without any limitations in time and space. And then its position in the prophetic context is a sign that it has been raised to a new level of assertion. It had to lose its rather material and earthly ring, or at least lessen the value of such an implication, to remain adaptable to the higher level of prophetic utterance. Hence as used by Micheas, all boundaries linked to place and time which had hitherto kept 'peace' within well-defined co-ordinates now disappear. Placed in a new context, and referred to the totally changed relationship between Yahweh and all the nations of the End of Days, the very same words as used in Micheas 4:4 transcend all limitations and now serve to express comprehensively an eternal and universal peace. The passage of the prophecy in question is proved to be eschatological by the concluding words of its introduction. And now Micheas 4:4 sums up the promise of the fully manifest Kingdom of God which is given in Micheas 4:1-3. In a similarly intensified assertion, from which all limitations have been removed, the 'nomadic' citation describes the final period of salvation in Zacharias 3:10.

These different fashions of applying the saying about peace in 3 Kings 5:5 also make it plain that peace will only become fully real in the eschatological fulfilment. Hence the hope of final peace is an essential part of Old

Testament eschatology, or better, in the eschatological expectations of the Old Testament the final period of peace is already presupposed. Important for our considerations is the fact that the same words are used for a preliminary and limited type of peace, as for the description of the definitive and unlimited peaceful joy.

It would be very strange if the route which these three elements of Old Testament revelation have taken were not also perceptible in the most central theological utterance of the Old Testament, namely in the way in which the Covenant is depicted and realized. But the Covenant too, as follows at once with inner logic and indeed necessity from the general eschatological direction of the Old Testament revelation, is embedded in a similar movement of development; and this movement may likewise be grasped and explained by the principle of literary form and tradition which we have called 'transposing of motifs'.

Here we may prescind from a general consideration of what a covenant is, and from a more precise treatment of the Covenant with Noah (Gen 9:8-17), since this is considered valid for all humanity of all ages and brings all men into a certain relationship to God. This Covenant confirms creation in its earthly constitution. And this confirmation receives the highest guarantee, that of God, since it comes in the solemn form of a Covenant based on natural grounds. Does this not suggest the conclusion, or at least the well-founded opinion, that the creative act of God itself has already come in the form of a Covenant, in the same way as the preservation of the world is guaranteed by the Covenant with Noah after the Flood? Should we not be able to find the same type of divine action in creation, in the creative activity of God and in the effects of his action, as we find in the granting of the Covenant?

We have to begin here too with Abraham, as we did when investigating the first motif, that of religious 'wandering'. According to the universally observed principle that God's action leaves lasting traces behind it, this new intervention of God takes place with regard to Abraham. The act of divine election (Gen 12:1–3) is transferred into the state of election. This new state of election is given vivid expression and realization in the Covenant with Abraham. Twice, in Genesis 15 and 17, the giving of the Covenant is narrated. This fact alone, that one single account is not exhaustive, is indicative of the outstanding significance of this Covenant, which is the first *supernatural* one of the Old Testament.

Coming to details, we may distinguish four essential elements of this Covenant.

1) In the Covenant, a new relationship is established between God and Abraham. It is no longer restricted to the general providence of God for all men, of which God had already assured all mankind for all time after they had escaped from the Flood, when speaking to Noah (Gen 9:15–17). Rather, the election and the covenant at the beginning of Abraham's new life with and before God, single him out from the mass of mankind at the time, and put him into a position of special closeness to God. He who has to live close to God can only do it when he is close to God in his being also. The Covenant then gives Abraham the power of receiving divine apparitions, and makes him worthy of them (Gen 18). Indeed, through the Covenant, he is raised to the level of a friend of God (Gen 18:17 ff).

2) This new relationship of Abraham to God is not something accidental, granted only at intervals to the elect.

It is rather something fundamental, based on an enduring state, on a new way of being in Abraham. This finds expression in Genesis 15:6 in a form which became classical: 'It was reckoned to him as justification'. Before all the theological speculation and division of opinion to which this saying later gave rise, the assertion is made thereby that Abraham is given his proper place in a relation of fellowship. (This is the broad, original meaning of the biblical 'justification', which must always therefore be further specified by an indication of the fellowship in question.) In the framework of the newly-installed economy of divine salvation, it cannot mean a well-ordered relationship which embraces only men. Here it clearly means the relation of fellowship with God into which the man Abraham enters. Justification therefore means in this text that Abraham is 'just' in the eyes of God, that is, 'right': he is what he should be. He abides before God in his whole personal being, in consequence of which he must possess a new quality of being which attracts God's good pleasure to him. By this new way of being, he bears within himself the competence and the possibility of making a reality of God's promise, 'Thou shalt be a blessing' (Gen 12:2).

3) The Covenant is made public in the sign of the Covenant. According to Genesis 17:9-14, the Covenant with Abraham is announced in public by the sign of circumcision. We need of course not go into the origin of this rite. According to Genesis 17, God chose this well-known sign, which was widely practised in the Near East, to reveal the Covenant outwardly. Thereby he proclaimed that the body of the elect has also been taken into the relationship set up by the Covenant, and hence that the Covenant binds Abraham and his heirs in their whole human being. From the point of view of the Patriarch, this

sign of the Covenant is likewise an external confession that Yahweh is the only God. In it too Abraham pronounces his perceptible 'yes' to his election and to the divine revelations.

4) Finally, essential to the Covenant are the set of obligations which arise from it. The divine obligation is contained in the promise to bestow on Abraham a great number of descendants and to give the land of Canaan as heritage. Just as the sign of the Covenant, circumcision, is the outward acceptance of the duties of the Covenant, the positive response to the self-revelation of God, so too it must take place inwardly in faith (Gen 15:6). It would certainly be incorrect to suppose here an already developed faith, understood in the dogmatic sense. But it must be noted that in the faith of Abraham we are dealing not merely with an intellectual attitude. It is something which takes in the whole man. It means therefore an attitude which claims the whole personality: Abraham gives up all earthly assurances and henceforth reassures himself only in faith, relying only on God, whom he knows thanks to the revelation which he has been granted, whom he now acknowledges, and to whom he now commits himself. He 'affirms himself', as von Rad says, in the God who discloses himself to him at present, and who will start from him to realize in the future his plan for the salvation of men, a plan which is to direct all history.

What happened to Abraham was a sort of sign-post. It received a new, intensive fulness of reality when it reached the level of the Covenant of God with the Twelve Tribes of Israel on Sinai. Here too the law of 'transposing of motifs' is palpable. On a different level and in a different sort of realization at a newer, higher stage of reality, the Covenant is given on Sinai, though in and according to the structure laid down in the Covenant with Abraham. Eichrodt expresses as follows the peculiar relation between the two covenants: 'The Covenant with Abraham and the Covenant on Sinai showed themselves as two mutually co-ordinated events which could be regarded as "Prelude" and "Fulfilment"; they give Israel's history its peculiar stamp of being directed by God' (W. Eichrodt, *Theology of the Old Testament,* Vol. I [Philadelphia, Pa.: West-minster, 1961]).

In the Covenant on Sinai we can remark the same essential elements as in the earlier one, *mutatis mutandis.*

1) The Covenant brings about a new relationship to God. It had been granted to Israel to experience the special nearness of God's providence—in anticipation as it were of the Covenant—in the two-fold presence of God, both in the pillar of fire and the pillar of cloud, and also in the form of the Angel of Yahweh during the Exodus (Ex 13:21; 14:19). On Sinai it is then granted to Israel to be witness of the coming of Yahweh, though in due distance with regard to the inapproachable holiness of God (Ex 19:17; 24:17). The nearness of God, henceforth dwelling among them (Num 23:21), makes of Israel a people set apart from all other peoples (Num 23:9; see also 2 Sam 7:23 f), a people which can no longer be compared with any other.

2) It is hardly open to doubt that this nearness to God cannot be but a passing quality. It contains rather, as a permanent attribute, what the announcement of its election (Ex 19:5 f) put before the covenanting people: that it should be 'God's special acquisition, a kingdom of priests and a holy people'. It means in other words a new way of being before God, which affects the whole people. The people united to God in the Covenant is a holy people,

enjoying as such the friendship and the grace of God. On this basis, then, a set of legal duties can be urged, with the appeal for holiness of life. (So for instance in Ex 22:30; Lev 11:44 f; 19:2; 20:26; 21:8.)

3) The sacrifice mentioned in Exodus 24 is not only a sign of extraordinary solemnity. Being essentially the sacrifice of the Covenant, it is so intrinsically linked with the Covenant on Sinai that the term 'Covenant' can be used simply for this sacrifice in Exodus 24:8. In the divine service of each day and feast, the sacrifice according to the Old Testament has the function of manifesting the permanent validity of the Covenant for Israel, and of making it present and actual in all its salvific effects. It is precisely the function of the daily sacrifice (*Tamid*) to re-vivify every day anew the exodus from Egypt and the granting of the Covenant (Num 28:6 ff; Deut 16:6). In the sacrifice, Israel is favoured each day with the possibility of renewing the attitude of the Covenant and of making its own the graces of salvation therein contained. This throws light on the function which falls to the renewal of the Covenant (as in Jos 24).

4) What God obliges himself to is contained in the extraordinary manifestation of grace which is guaranteed to Israel in the proclamation of election uttered by Yahweh himself (Ex 19:3-6). Indeed, according to Exodus 20:5 f, that is according to the promise attached to the first commandment of the Decalogue, God's grace and mercy are far more the determining factor in his relation to the people of the Covenant than is his punitive justice.

The duty of the other partner to the Covenant, Israel, may be simply determined as the obligation to keep the whole of the Law (Ex 19:8; 24:3-7). In the final editing of the Book of Exodus, the proclamation of the election by God (Ex 19) and the Covenant (Ex 24), are the frame which encloses the Decalogue and the Book of the Covenant (Ex 20-23). This gives expression to the fact that the Law has merely a functional significance for the persistence of Israel in the Covenant. The Law is, as it were, a by-product. The pillars on which Israel is based are the election and the Covenant, the free gift of God's plan of salvation, which precedes all Israel's own achievement. The Law itself therefore only fulfils its function when, as God's living directive, it constantly points to him. Under no circumstances may it be erected into something absolute in its own right, as did the Pharisees, according to John 19:7.

Later, in contrast to the historical reality, the promise of the New Covenant appears on an essentially higher level in the progress of revelation (Jer 31:31-34; 32:37-42). And yet the persistence of the term 'covenant' would alone be a sufficient warning not to suppose that here is something totally novel. Here too, using 'transposition of motif' as a principle of interpretation, one can most effectively separate the progressive development from the permanent basic structure and show the meaning of the elements on either side. The basic structure may be recognized at once by the sameness of the formulation of the Covenant: 'I will be their God and they shall be my people' (Jer 31:33; 32:38).

1) In the future salvation, the relationship to God will be very close, because then he will speak to his partner in the Covenant heart to heart, and adapt him entirely to himself. He will take away from the heart of his people their previous vacillation, and turn their heart of stone into a heart of flesh (Ez 36:24-28). He will renew the spirit

of the people, strengthen it, and make it firm in God
(Ps. 51:12).

2) The new way of being, for those who belong to God,
is described in Jeremias 31:32 by the image of the closest
union in the fellowship of marriage. It is therefore seen
as a total claim by God on the whole human personality.
The Covenant with Abraham and the Covenant on Sinai
had already made it clear that this new way of being before
and with God was no static condition, but meant at once
a dynamic movement towards God. This higher and more
intensive form of existence along with God in the promised
New Covenant is penetrated through and through and
transformed by the fire of the supremely dominant love
of God. And to this love, because God 'speaks to the heart'
(Os 2:16), because the innermost kernel of the human
person is embraced, a corresponding loving answer, in word
and action, is given by man.

3) The sign of this Covenant is no longer a mere external reminder, but the heart itself, a heart newly-created
within, entirely directed to God and constantly holding
him present. Such is the distinguishing sign of this new
and eternal Covenant (Jer 31:33; 32:40).

4) The obligation to observe God's will is no longer felt
by man in the New Covenant as something alien to him
and imposed on him from outside. It is placed within him
and there perceived as something fitting to man and as
the expression of the selfless love of God. This new way
in which obligation exists is then something to which the
partner in the Covenant responds spontaneously and freely,
because the rule of the distant God has become the
autonomy of the present God of the Covenant, towards
whom the heart, a new creation, is drawn as towards a
magnetic field of forces.

But in spite of all progressive development, the New Covenant remains in essential continuity with the Old. It is realized more brightly and clearly, more comprehensively and effectively, but within the framework which God first set up in the historical covenants, especially the Covenant of Sinai. Its basis is therefore elastic and strong enough to take upon it the fulfilment of the New Testament. From this New Testament, in its fulfilment, will then proceed the eschatological covenant of friendship, or better, this New and Eternal Covenant will in the Last Days manifest itself as the eschatological covenant of friendship with God, which according to Isaias 25:6-8, unites God's own with God in a festal meal, in closest fellowship.

Starting from different points, the lines traced by the motifs of pilgrimage, Sion, peace and above all Covenant, which are brought to the forefront at telling points of the development of revelation in the Old Testament, come together in the glorious prophecies of Isaias 2:2-4; Micheas 4:1-4; Isaias 25:6-8, with their promises for the End. They reveal themselves as different essential elements for the realization of the same eschatological Kingdom of God. The sacred writers, when describing it, turn back on historical data and employ earthly themes, which they then perfect and raise to a higher level, in the further course of development of revelation. One reason for this is that they had to evoke this Kingdom in some way that would be comprehensible to their contemporaries, unless they were to remain merely rhetorical. But the essential reason is that God, for the sake of his plan of setting up and realizing this Kingdom, set in movement a gradual, upward process of history, a unilinear direction towards a goal, which was pointed towards that august end and thus brought in with it an historical beginning. We say, 'unilinear', but it is not to be understood as a steeply ascending straight line. It is rather, in the manner of the geometric figure of a spiral, a line with breaks which, in spite of all the human discontinuity embraced by God's plans (see Gen 50:20), is transformed into a special kind of continuity in the process of salvation. This unity, and the historical development of the Old Testament faith which gains in clarity through the progress of revelation, is treated similarly by H. H. Rowley, in *The Faith of Israel* (Philadelphia: Westminster, 1957), p. 16: 'It is the unity of growth and not a static unity, and each stage of the growth must be considered in relation to the whole, as well as in its uniqueness . . . That unity is here conceived as the unity of the development of the distinctive faith of Israel. Within that faith there were incipient ideas and principles which became formulated with increasing clarity in due course'.

The first seminal steps on this way are already pregnant with an inner tension and dynamism which are directed towards this end. Hence the progress of revelation, even in the eschatological fulfilment, never leads to a total change in the previous order of things. From the historical starting-point on, the basic structure of the divine economy of salvation indicates the lines of development. And the lines of development, as they lead gradually upwards, retain the fundamental structure. We may refer here to J. van der Ploeg's 'Profetie en vervulling', in *Studia Catholica*, 1953, where he discusses the problem that God's promises are often fulfilled differently from the way men expect from the words of the prophecy. Still, taken in general, the prophetic word has an understandable meaning for its first hearers also. It was not uttered in vain to them: 'It clearly indicated the direction in which God willed to lead people and individuals'.

The main interest of our present essay is to illustrate this direction by some examples. The nature and manner of the eschatological fulfilment, and the direction in which it is accomplished, are therefore given beforehand in the primary events of revelation as they are tangible in the history of Israel. And they are pointed out and defined as Old Testament prophecy constantly comes back to them in the process of its evolution. Hence the future goal of hope remains within the framework of what was already laid down, the divine plan which is made visible in the history of salvation. And the hope is closely linked to the history. The goal is disclosed as the reality of an ideal world, which is indeed transformed, but within and in keeping with the original basic structure.

All explanations of the eschatological passages of the Old Testament must bear this in mind if they are not to drift too far from the original data of revelation, as they could in a spiritual or symbolical interpretation which has lost touch with the facts. From the very beginning, the promises of the final Kingdom tend towards this 'ideal reality' which grows ever clearer. The promises, even as distant image and faint suspicion, are already tied to their own type, and at each stage of their progress they allow their essential quality to shine through in its proper light.

Here it is well to discuss briefly a principle of interpretation which is coming more and more to the forefront in French-speaking countries. This is the so-called *'relecture biblique'*, the re-reading of the Bible, which seems to be related to the 'transposition of motifs' described above. This type of interpretation was introduced into exegesis by the Old Testament scholar of Lyons, E. Podechard. His successor, A. Gelin, who has made particular use of it, would prefer to call it 're-interpretation'.

The object of this method is to distinguish the additions made at different times to biblical passages from the original contents, and to recognize them as the 'graftings' of later but still biblical times. Such additions would have been made in order to render the original texts capable of meeting the changes brought about by new historical situations. Gelin gives as example, Psalm 47 among others, which was first understood historically and later eschatologically; also Psalm 22, which was first uttered as a psalm containing a vow by an individual 'poor man', and later given a messianic turn in line with the Servant Song of Isaias 53. The Greek translation, the Septuagint, provides a new 're-reading' for many texts, for instance Genesis 3 : 15, Isaias 7 : 14. Finally, as Gelin understands the matter, Christ, in a last and definitive 're-reading', relates the Old Testament to himself and his task and gives it its uttermost fulfilment. H. Cazelles, in *À la rencontre de Dieu*, has recently given an exegesis of Psalm 29 according to this method.

There is certainly an unmistakable resemblance in the methods, but there is also an essential difference which must not be overlooked. The 're-reading' of the Bible draws on the rich and inexhaustible content of biblical passages—whose sense is never merely of the past, but always actual and fertile, always opening on bottomless depths—and can disassociate them from their former historical situations, with the help of changes and additions of a greater or lesser extent, which were made under the influence of inspiration. It can thus allot them various new historical situations, and so let them have, in the course of Old Testament revelation, an ever-actual force, and see them as vehicles of the future. In this process the same texts consequently show on later occasions a higher level of the development of revelation, in contrast to the original.

The 'transposition of motifs', on the other hand, implies that a certain theme is taken over from a given passage in the Bible, that under certain circumstances its limits in time and space are removed, that it is inserted into a later passage, and that in this process it receives and expresses a fuller content. The same motif therefore remains open and receptive for a more developed stage of revelation. The sameness of the motif points therefore to the inner dynamism and direction of revelation, and so gives expression to something which cannot be ascribed without more ado to the 're-reading' of the Bible.

From all this it seems that the theology of the Old Testament has the task of giving due consideration to the development, intrinsic to the Bible, of such dominant themes which can be followed by means of 'transposition of motifs'. It has the task of presenting objectively the intrinsic and essential connexions between the reality of revelation in history and the eschatological fulfilment in expectation. This is the task which is indicated and demanded by the frequent 'transposition of motifs' in the Old Testament, a process which can often be proved to have taken place, and of which only a few examples have been selected here.

Franz
Mussner

THE HISTORICAL JESUS AND
THE CHRIST OF FAITH

The Gospels are explanations of the history of Jesus. They do not give a 'neutral' account of the life of Jesus of Nazareth. We have rather four men who live in the conviction of faith that Jesus is the salvation of the world, and who see in his history what gives meaning to their own history. So in the Gospels, and even earlier in the 'Gospel before the Gospels', we certainly have a history of Jesus which has been adapted to the kerygma, the proclamation of salvation. In view of our theme we must say, even more precisely, that the historical Jesus in the Gospel tradition is never seen otherwise than with the eyes of faith. There is also the fact that apart from the New Testament sources for the history of Jesus, we have only very scanty testimonies about him elsewhere. Pliny, Tacitus, Flavius Josephus, the Talmud—from these hardly anything can be derived beyond the sheer fact of his existence.

It follows necessarily from all this that we can reach the historical Jesus only through the medium of the account

of him contained in the New Testament, and which was
written in the service of the kerygma. But this conclusion
brings with it the question: Do we then reach the historical Jesus at all? Or do we meet everywhere, no matter
where we take up the Gospels, only the Christ of faith,
that is to say, only a figure of history which has already
been given this or that interpretation? And when we do
reach the Jesus of history, what has he to do with the
'Christ of faith'? Are the two figures essentially the same,
or is there in fact a discontinuity between them?

Ever since Martin Kähler's lecture on 'The So-called
Historical Jesus and the Biblical Christ of Faith', in which
he called for a new approach to the question, the matter
has been much discussed in Protestant theology. First
published in 1892, the lecture was published again (in its
revised form of 1896) in 1953, at Munich. The discussion
has been particularly lively in recent years, and is reflected
for instance in J. M. Robinson's *New Quest for the Historical Jesus,* (Naperville, Illinois: Allenson, 1959). Since
the problem exists and represents a real problem, Catholic
theology must face it seriously and try to give an answer
to the above-mentioned questions, even though the question of the 'Jesus of history' has to some extent an unhappy
pre-history, especially in French-speaking regions, in which
it is linked with the name of A. Loisy. The debate he was
engaged in, however, laid emphasis on other points than
those of to-day.

Kähler's famous lecture was inspired first and foremost
by attack and defence against the 'liberal' research into
the life of Jesus in the eighteenth and nineteenth centuries,
where the search for the historical Jesus had led to a radical
destruction of the 'Christ of faith'. Kähler saw—correctly,
as everyone agrees to-day—that this destruction, paradoxi-

cally enough, brought to light a 'historical Jesus' who often had little or nothing to do with the historical Jesus who is met in the pages of the Gospels.

Kähler looked at these products of a highly subjective interpretation, and recognized in them so many attacks on the foundations of the Christian faith. Now, Kähler was well aware of the peculiar nature of the Gospel story of Jesus, though he was too early on the scene to know anything about 'form-criticism' of the Gospels. He could say: 'We possess no sources for a life of Jesus which historical research would accept as reliable and sufficient. I underline: for a biography of Jesus of Nazareth according to the standards of to-day's historical research'. He did not therefore try to prove more or less the identity of the historical Jesus with the Christ of faith by historical methods. He took squarely the stand-point of the Gospels themselves: the Christ of faith whom they proclaim *is* the historical Jesus and no one else! Kähler rejected all efforts to distil from the Gospels a so-called historical Jesus with the help of historical methods which seemed to him questionable. His refusal was based on the peculiar nature of historical writing in the Gospels. Since the Gospels are 'Testimonies of faith', it was, Kähler thought, impossible to recognize a 'historical Jesus' *besides* the Christ of faith. The 'real' historical Jesus is rather that Christ whom biblical faith confesses. It is impossible and also unnecessary to get behind this faith.

To this solution of the problem W. Herrmann long ago made the objection: 'The fact is that in the New Testament Christ is so proclaimed as he is seen by faith. Consequently, this proclamation, if we surrender ourselves to it, cannot of itself guard us from the doubt that we are trying to base our faith on something which is perhaps not historical fact at all, but the product of faith' (*Zeitschrift für Theologie und Kirche*, 1892).

The objection is justified. For faith seeks a foundation in history, and not merely in preaching and creeds. Hence the question of the historical Jesus cannot be dismissed by a reference to the peculiar nature of the Gospel story of Jesus. Rather, in spite of this peculiarity, we must seriously put the question: Do we reach the historical Jesus in the Gospels? Are there any criteria which make a positive answer to the question possible? Notice that it is not a question of being able to reach 'some sort of' historical Jesus. That would take us no farther than the liberal research into the life of Jesus. The point is: Can we reach a historical Jesus, by means of exact historical methods, who has not merely 'something' to do with the Christ of faith, but has something essential to do with him? Our questions have grown still more acute than in Kähler's day, because meanwhile 'form-criticism', as it is called, has produced the proof that we have not in the Gospels a biography of Jesus in the modern sense of history. It has been proved that the Gospels, at least the Synoptics, are rather collections to a great extent, where smaller and larger pieces of tradition have been linked together by the Evangelists, acting as editors. We know, for instance, that St Mark's 'straightway' or St Matthew's 'then' are to be regarded simply as elements of the style of the editor, and not to be given strict 'biographical' value.

In addition, there is another result of form-criticism to be taken into account. The traditions worked over in the Gospels (the 'pericopes') often received their particular concrete 'forms' only in their individual '*Sitz im Leben*', social setting, in the primitive Church, that is, in the cult, in missionary preaching or in the primitive catechesis (instruction). Thus it would appear that form-critical work on the Gospels leads necessarily to scepticism with regard to the historical Jesus. Hence it is all the more necessary to look for criteria by whose help we can still reach the historical Jesus in the Gospels. In this effort, only those are to be mentioned to which even a critically-minded exegesis would not refuse its consent at once.

Criteria for the Historical Jesus in the Gospels

Such criteria have already been indicated again and again in the discussion of our subject. The best that has been written on it seems to be N. A. Dahl's 'Der historische Jesu als geschichtswissenschaftliches und theologisches Problem', in *Kerygma und Dogma*, Göttingen, 1955. Let us first therefore briefly sum up his criteria and clarify them a little (1–5) and then try to complete them with one more (6).

1) There is one absolutely certain starting-point, which can never be seriously denied as a historical fact. This is the violent death of Jesus on the cross.

2) With this historical fact of the *violent* death of Jesus, however, there is also given the assurance, historically, that Jesus made some special claim. Without such a claim, the catastrophe which ended his life would not be historically understandable. Whether his claim was to be the Messiah is a question which will not engage our attention for the moment. However, we may already point out that this question, quite apart from the testimony of the Gospels, must in fact be answered positively, and that on account of the specific history and expectations of the Jewish people. Dahl has later insisted on the *'titulus'* on the cross of Jesus, 'The King of the Jews'. This can derive

neither from the 'proof from prophecy' nor from the 'theology of the community'. The title shows that the messianic claim of Jesus played an important role, however perverted, in his trial. (See Mark 14:61 and the parallel texts.)

3) Jesus appears in the Gospels, from one end to the other, as an individual 'character' of a very marked type, whose uniqueness confronts us in the Synoptics as well as in St John. There are many traits which are precisely typical for him, and only for him, and which are distinctive. Such are his attitudes to various groups of his nation, to the Pharisees and their theology, to the tax-gatherers and 'sinners', to the poor. We observe in him a figure with a very marked manner of reaction, which is unique and inimitable. This 'character' cannot be fiction. As Dahl says, 'there is something distinctive about Jesus'. And this is true even of his words.

4) The 'world' in which Jesus lived points unmistakably to the land of Palestine. The Jesus we meet in the Gospels is one who lives in the milieu of late Judaism. This is obvious once more in the Synoptics as well as in St John. This milieu is not merely the background of Jesus' coming and of his work, especially of his preaching. It is in fact what makes his work possible. For instance, in the Hellenistic world outside Palestine, the controversy with the Pharisees, which leads to the heart of Jesus' preaching, could never have come to be. 'To a great extent the theology of the nineteenth century had no notion of what it meant that Jesus was a Jew in the full sense of the word and a member of his people. They sought in him a founder of a religion, or a saviour who would burst through the limits of Judaism and throw open the way to the "gentiles" . . . And yet the New Testament tradition is not

being taken seriously in its historical significance, when the Jewishness of Jesus, in the fullest sense, is not recognized' (O. Michel). Again, this controversy with the theology of the Pharisees forms the background of the message in many of Jesus' parables.

5) The historical Jesus also confronts us in the nature and manner of his preaching. It consists to a great extent of short, pregnant sentences, and is built up of characteristic episodes, which fix themselves easily in the memory. The systematic theologian does not speak in this way, but only the individual wisdom-teacher. The Apostle speaks differently from Jesus!

6) In a close investigation into various *sets* of sayings, in the Synoptic tradition, we often have to remark how inadequately the individual sayings have been worked into the composite production of the Evangelist. The collocation does not succeed in doing 'invisible mending', and the joins between the single sayings show the added threads. Within a given series, the sayings are not always 'logically' connected with each other. Sayings are often strung together merely on the basis of a common catchword, without any inner links being perceptible. We may therefore speak of an inadequate composition of sayings in the Synoptic Gospels. Examples of this would be for instance the pericope of the debate about rank (Mk 9:33-37) and parallels, as indeed the whole section Mark 9:33-50 is characteristic in this matter. Commenting on the section, R. Schnackenburg says: 'It is precisely in the fact that many rough edges are not smoothed out that we see how tied the Evangelists were to the data of tradition'. Indeed, one can go further. Here we see how the apostolic tradition about Jesus was tied to the voice of Jesus. No one dared, or only very rarely, either the Evangelist or the

Gospel before the Gospels, to modify the sayings of Jesus so strongly that it could have led to loss of the substance of the 'wisdom' he uttered. Too great reverence was felt for the words of the Master.

St Luke often shows himself a master in the collocation of sayings. For instance, in the section 13 : 22–30, he can compose something out of a series of separate sayings which actually results in a continuous parable story, although it is undoubtedly a posterior piece of construction. The links have been built up artificially, as I have shown in the *Trierer Theologische Zeitschrift*, 1956.

Indeed, reverence for the very voice of Jesus went so far that no one dared to eliminate the obscurity from dark and difficult sayings of Jesus, though efforts were made to interpret them by the aid of certain collocations. We have a classical example of this in the saying of Jesus which is transmitted by Mark 9 : 1 : 'Truly, truly, I say to you, there are some of those standing by who will not taste death till they see the Kingdom of God coming in power'. The inconsequential narrative of the Gospel then gives the account of the Transfiguration of Jesus, because it was believed that one could recognize in this event a sort of fulfilment of the promise of Jesus which the previous saying of Jesus contained. In reality, the saying in question is by no means fully and satisfactorily 'explained' by the Transfiguration. To this very day it remains still obscure. Nothing would have been handier than to modify the saying in such a way that the account of the Transfiguration would present in fact an adequate 'Fulfilment' of the promise as given in the saying. However, they shrank from doing this. They left the saying in its obscurity, apart from some modifications in its second half by the two other Synoptic Gospels, which also record it.

To sum up, we may say that there exists in fact a series of criteria which enable us to penetrate in the Gospels to the historical Jesus. If we once read the Gospels through, from this point of view, the 'material' for the historical Jesus will actually be very great.

But even if our search for such criteria is successful, we have not yet answered the question which arises necessarily from our subject: Why is the history of Jesus narrated at all in the Gospels? Why is something like a 'biography' of Jesus put forward?

The Interest of the New Testament in the History of Jesus

Did the apostolic preaching have any interest at all in the historical Jesus? It seems indeed that at first an interest was taken only in the two decisive factors of salvation, the death and resurrection of Jesus, and not at all in the details of his life. We prescind here from the old confessions of faith, preserved in fragments or short formulas in the New Testament epistles, and refer only to the ancient traditional material contained in the speeches of St Peter in the Acts of the Apostles, though it is not always possible to sift out that material in all its details. 'Here we certainly have ancient matter, which undoubtedly goes back to the first Christian community at Jerusalem' (E. Schweizer).

The first thing that strikes us is that he in whom those Christians believed, to whom they prayed, is not called 'Lord' or 'Saviour' or the like, but always 'Jesus', or 'Jesus of Nazareth' (Acts 2:22; 3:6; 4:10; 6:14; 10:38). The interest of faith is therefore directed to a concrete historical figure who goes by the name of Jesus of Nazareth. Acts 2:22 proclaims this Jesus of Nazareth as a man whom 'God attested to you by means of mighty works and wonders and signs, which God wrought through him among you'. Here we find already a modest reference to the life of Jesus on earth, before Easter. In the preaching of St Peter, as recorded in Acts 10: 34-43, the proclamation concerning Jesus is further enlarged to take in definite data and stages of his life. The activity of the Baptist is mentioned, Galilee is named as the starting-point of the public activity of Jesus, his working of miracles is once more referred to, and likewise his companions are referred to as witnesses of his work. Only then follows the reference to his violent death and his resurrection. And the Kerygma proper—note here the term, 'proclaim'—follows only in verse 42: 'This is he whom God has made Judge of the living and the dead!' The pronoun 'this' gives the unity of the historical Jesus with the Christ of faith. But even if one were to see in this sermon of St Peter in the house of Cornelius a product of St Luke's pen—which is hardly correct, as at least a traditional basic outline must be assumed for the structure of the discourse—yet the question still remains: Why such interest in the historical Jesus in a *sermon*, which sets out to proclaim what is of decisive import about the 'Christ of faith'? A series of reasons may be given in reply.

1) In the apostolic preaching, the death of Jesus on the cross is not merely proclaimed as a factor of salvation, it is recorded as a historical fact. But if this is so, the cross of Jesus comes into a chain of causality, to which clearly even the apostolic community is not quite indifferent. The primitive apostolic preaching gives two causes for the death of Jesus. One is the ostensible historical one: the act of the Jews and the godless heathens, who brought Jesus to the cross. (See Acts 2: 23*b*; 3: 13-15; 4: 27; 5: 30; 10: 39*b*; 13: 28.) The other is 'in the background and

supra-historical': the will of God, already revealed in the Scriptures. (See Acts 2:23*a*; 3:18; 4:28; 13:27*b*; 1 Cor 15:3.) Why then is the apostolic preaching not content with the mere Kerygma, something like: 'Christ died for us and rose again; you are saved, if you believe in him'? Why must it bring the proclamation of salvation into a causal connexion with the historical processes of the death of Jesus, and with the will of God which is revealed in the Old Testament?

First, it would appear, for apologetic reasons, to guard against objections which could be brought against his messiahship in spite of the announcement of his resurrection from the dead, the *scandalum crucis*. For 'the passion and death of Jesus, regarded as the death of the Messiah, was in irreconcilable opposition to the messianic hopes of the Jewish people of the time' (J. Gewiess). But an 'explanation' of the death of Jesus was needed not merely for the Jews. Even converts to Christianity from paganism wanted to know how the violent death of him whom we revere as our Lord could ever have taken place. This, the apostolic preaching had to answer.

The answer was to present the death of Jesus, on the one hand, as having taken place 'according to the Scriptures' and hence corresponding to the will of God. The self-interpretation of the Risen Lord played its part in this. And on the other hand, the preaching recounted how the death of Jesus came about from the point of view of history. *This led necessarily to the telling of the history of Jesus,* especially the events which had led up to the fatal clash of Jesus with his opponents. This did not immediately demand a connected narrative of the life of Jesus. It sufficed at first to give the narrative of characteristic situations, to recall certain 'challenging' and 'exigent' sayings, to recount controversies, to give parables which contained clearly enough, though in a veiled manner, the claims of Jesus, and then the story of the Passion itself. At first therefore an 'anecdotal narrative' (O. Michel) was enough. But a certain modest effort at a connected 'biography' of Jesus was present very early, as Acts 10: 37-40 shows. The drama of the passion of Jesus needed some expounding. M. Kähler said long ago in his lecture, speaking of the Gospels: 'Somewhat daringly, one could call them Passion Narratives with long introductions'. This formulation stems from a correct piece of observation, though it does not name the one reason why as early as the primitive Church an interest was taken in the history of Jesus. But we already see that the apostolic proclamation of salvation itself, telling of the death and resurrection of Jesus, cried out for the history of Jesus, if it were not to remain in a space devoid of history and be understood as myth. Jesus died no 'accidental' death. This death had its causes, which had to be given.

2) The vital interest of the New Testament in the historical Jesus is also connected with the fact that Jesus of Nazareth is proclaimed in the New Testament as the *decisive eschatological event*. Even E. Käsemann, who considers as 'community kerygma' every text of the New Testament 'in which any sort of messianic predicate appears', thinks that no Old Testament prophet had 'the eschatological importance' which 'Jesus clearly attributed to his actions'. For this he refers to the 'much-discussed' saying in Matthew 11: 12 f, with the comment: 'Jesus thought that with his words the Kingdom came to his hearers'. And even if one thinks, with Käsemann, that Jesus did not 'preach the realized reign of God . . . but only a reign which comes into effect from now on', still,

this 'from now on' implies at once a Christology, and Bultmann's view that the significance of Jesus as Messiah and Son of Man 'does not lie at all in what he did in the past, but in what was expected from him in the future', demands to be revised.

For a proper grasp of the eschatological consciousness of Jesus, we are also referred to some antitheses in the Sermon on the Mount. M. Dibelius was right indeed in saying that the Sermon on the Mount shows 'no strongly delineated Christology'. Still he does not hesitate to explain the fact that the Sermon on the Mount has 'gained authority over millions of men', by the circumstance that 'it was Jesus who proclaimed these sayings'. Käsemann, who maintains the authenticity of the first, second and fourth antitheses, emphasizes quite rightly 'that with the words "But I say unto you", the speaker claims an authority which stands on the same level as, and goes against, the authority of Moses. But one who claims an authority on the same level as, or which opposes that of Moses, has in fact placed himself above Moses and ceased to be a Rabbi. The Jew who does what is done here has either broken with the community of Judaism or he brings the messianic Law, and that is the Messiah'. Hence he concludes: 'The only category which does justice to his claim is completely independent of whether he himself used it and demanded it or not. It is the category which his disciples then attributed to him in fact, that of the Messiah'.

Among the sayings, therefore, attributed to Jesus by the Gospel tradition, there is a whole series which must be recognized as authentic even by a critical exegesis, and which at least imply a Christology. That they entered at all into the tradition appears also to be connected with

14

the fact that the apostolic preaching could use them to demonstrate splendidly the unity of the 'Christ of faith' and the historical Jesus.

In this connexion we must also refer to Mark 1: 15 ('The time is fulfilled and the Reign of God is at hand'), a saying which St Mark seems to have taken as the head-line for his 'Gospel of Jesus Christ' (Mk 1: 1). As a literary form, it must be designated as a 'Herald's Cry'. Note the verbs 'fulfilled' and 'is at hand' which are used to end the sentences, with their strikingly kerygmatic tone. The assertions of this cry are in the perfect. That means, in the context in which the saying is placed in the Gospel, that the time is fulfilled, the moment has come, for now the Reign of God is immediately at the door. At the same time, the reign of Satan is already shattered, and through none other than Jesus (see Mk 1: 23–26). 'A new doctrine full of power! And he commanded the unclean spirits, and they obeyed him. And news of him went out at once in the whole region of Galilee' (1: 27 f). What Jesus pro-claimed as 'the good news from God' is the dawn of God's reign, and by virtue of the very fact that he, the Messiah, is there and at work.

The conviction of faith that Jesus was the decisive eschatological event, a conviction arising from the preach-ing of the historical Jesus, appears very particularly to have furthered interest in his historical life. (Here then also appear the limits of the view which would see the Gospel as a 'prolonged passion narrative'.) St Mark does not put the cart before the horse! For him the 'beginning' of 'the Good News of Jesus Christ' is not at the cross and resurrection of Jesus, but coincides with the beginning of his public ministry, and therefore with his baptism in the Jordan (Mk 1: 1 ff). The kerygma of the Passion was not given out in isolation, but obviously very early, along with the pre-Easter activity of Jesus, 'beginning from Galilee after the baptism which John preached' (Acts 10:37). 'Since then the "Beginning" of the Gospel does not take place only at the confession of faith and the preaching of the post-Easter community, but starts with the historical Jesus, the question of the beginning is one of the most important themes in New Testament theology' (E. Lohse). But if Jesus understood himself as the eschatological event, then what followed was perfectly legitimate. In the apostolic preaching the bringer of the message became the message, the historical Jesus became the Christ of faith.

If this is correct, then Bultmann is wrong in the opinion mentioned above, that the significance of Jesus, as Messiah and Son of Man, does not lie at all in what Jesus had done in the past. It is rather the other way round. It is precisely what the historical Jesus did that made it possible to proclaim him to the world as Messiah and Son of Man. Käsemann remarks: 'Because primitive Christianity experienced the earthly history of Jesus so intensely as "the Time", it wrote Gospels, and even after Easter it did not simply leave the story of Jesus at the mercy of all-comers'. What was this 'Time'? According to Bultmann, it was Jesus' call for decision, in which the proximity of the Reign of God is proclaimed (see his *Theology of the New Testament*, New York, 1951, p. 4 ff). But how does it come about that Jesus 'in his own person [is] the demand for decision', as even Bultmann admits? Only 'insofar as his call is God's last word before the end, and as such, calls for the decision' (*Ibid.*, 8)? Why then does Jesus link the decision so radically to his own person, as for instance happens clearly in the saying of Jesus (which Bultmann also recognizes as genuine): 'He who comes to me and does not hate father and mother, wife and children, brothers and sisters, yes and himself also, cannot be my disciple'? (Lk 14:26, and parallels). Here it is a matter, to put the point sharply, of Jesus and not of God! (We may add that Jesus' call for decision, as Bultmann understands it, the proclamation of the nearness of the Reign of God, but without messianic claim on the part of Jesus, would hardly have led to his violent death.)

If in the call for decision, uttered by Jesus, only the Kingdom of *God* was meant, Jesus could not have linked the decision so closely to his own person. For 'the word expresses sharply the exclusiveness of Jesus' claim' (Fr. Hauck). And Bultmann's polemics against the messiahship attributed to Jesus by the community (in his *Theology of the New Testament*, New York: Scribners, p. 26 ff) fail of their effect, because Jesus could not interpret his mission in the light of the traditional messianic expectations. There was no unified traditional concept of the Messiah. His own messianic interpretation of his mission is to a great extent a new interpretation and a 'transformation' (Riesenfeld) of the old messianic tradition. (And we may note that a similar process may be observed already taking place within the Old Testament, and more particularly in the whole field of eschatology.) This new interpretation of the concept of Messiah on the part of Jesus, with the transformations it involved, was already necessary because he had also transformed the notion of the Reign of God. This is particularly clear in his parables of the Kingdom of God, in which however we have before us 'a piece of bedrock of tradition' (J. Jeremias). It was precisely at this new interpretation of the concept of Messiah and Kingdom of God that his opponents took scandal. In it we encounter in special measure the historical Jesus. In the apostolic preaching this transformation and new interpretation is merely taken up. But the 'call to decision' alone was far from implying any Christology. That was much more the connexion of Jesus' call to his own person, a link fraught with claims as with destiny.

3) Further, the desire to collect the exhortatory sayings of Jesus, as appears primarily in that stratum of tradition known as Q in exegesis, can only be explained satisfactorily if Jesus of Nazareth was recognized as more than a mere Jewish teacher of wisdom. Apparently this material, mostly discourse, functioned first and foremost not as a collection of wise sayings alongside of other traditions, but in place of another tradition, namely, the Jewish rabbinical 'Tradition of the Fathers'. So G. Kittel says, 'The isolation of the tradition of Jesus is constitutive of the Gospel'—a most important piece of insight! The sayings of Jesus did not gain the status of a Messianic Law only in the Gospel of St Matthew. They were collected for this very reason and, as it appears, in Jewish-Christian circles their author was regarded as the *messianic* teacher of the Community.

4) Faith is not content with a pure kerygma; it will have historical 'certainty' for the matters in which it has been instructed (see Lk 1:4). 'This clinging to history is one way of expressing the fact that salvation is *extra nos*' (Käsemann), something outside and independent of us. This objective quality of salvation is a necessary presupposition of faith, which cannot be renounced. With regard to the 'Christ of faith', it is attained precisely by recourse to the historical Jesus. The kerygma, and the faith which responds to the message, are founded on *history*. Otherwise the kerygma remains irrelevant.

5) Has the Gospel of St John also an interest in the

historical Jesus? Is it not rather 'an imaginative story about Jesus'? In any case, history and kerygma, reminiscence of the eye-witness and meditation of the author, inter-penetrate each other there to such an extent that to separate them is often no longer possible, or only at the cost of great effort. The richness of place-names (about thirty-three concrete indications) in this 'spiritual' Gospel is already something remarkable. But in the context of our theme, another observation is far more important. It is that the Gospel of St John takes an absolutely passionate interest in the heavenly redeemer's *becoming flesh*. That comes in fact to the same thing as a particular interest in the historical Jesus. Why did St John write a Gospel at all? Or, to put it more clearly, when the writing of Gospels had apparently been finished for thirty years, why did he put forward his interests once more precisely *in the form of a Gospel*? Because he wanted to oppose his *'Christus praesens'* to the Jesus of the Church's Synoptic tradition? Did he write, therefore, in a spirit of contradiction? Yes, he did—but not in opposition to the orthodox tradition about Jesus, but rather against a docetic-gnostic watering-down of the Christian kerygma! The epistles of St John are themselves enough to make that clear. In them he contends for the identity of (the historical) Jesus with the heavenly redeemer.

The heresies against which the epistles are directed cannot be reduced to any single formula such as 'docetism', as R. Schnackenburg has pointed out in his commentary. Their aspects are manifold. All the same, the author is fighting against 'a single front', since the false doctrine is concerned above all with Christology, and the contested views are orientated in the direction of gnosticism. The confession of faith in Christ, as it was traditional in the

Church, rests on the unity of the historical Jesus and the Christ of faith. Thus in the first Epistle of St John, 'Jesus is the Christ' (2:22; 5:1); 'Jesus is the Son of God' (4:15; 5:5); 'Jesus Christ who has come in flesh' (4:2); 'This—Jesus—is he who comes through water and blood' (5:6). But the heretics refuse to accept this confession of faith, and that leads to 'dissolving Jesus', that is to a destructive attack on the historical Jesus. This is the 'real work of Anti-Christ', as Harnack has well put it, on the basis of 1 John 4:3. The heresy is not concerned to deny a heavenly redeemer, but the incarnation of the redeemer in *Jesus of Nazareth*. This leads consequently to a dissolution of Christian soteriology, since in it the real 'flesh' of Jesus is rejected as a means of expiation. For this reason, St John lays this great emphasis, in contrast to the heretics, on the incarnation of the redeemer, and especially on the historical reality of his redeeming blood (see 1 Jn 5:6 ff; Jn 1:14; 6:53-56; 19:34).

The struggle is for the historical Jesus and his significance to the world as its saviour. And this was probably the real reason why St John put forward his theological interests, against the heretics, in the form of a 'Life of Our Lord', as well as in his epistles, although the writing of Gospels seemed to have been closed long before. Undoubtedly the Gospel of St John presents a completely new re-casting of the history of Jesus. But this is not done in opposition to previous gospel writing. It was done because the historical situation of the Church demanded a specialized type of interpretation of the life of Jesus, in which the last eye-witness of the 'glory' of the divine and heavenly Word, as it was manifested in the incarnate Jesus of Nazareth, was to put this glory before men's minds (see Jn 1:14). The indissoluble unity of the historical Jesus and the Christ of Glory is now to be demonstrated, and the task is raised to the level of a programme. In John 20:31, the preliminary ending of the Gospel, the object is stated clearly: 'These things are written, that you may believe that *Jesus* is the Christ, the Son of God'. The accent is on 'Jesus', and not on 'the Christ'. St John was well aware that the 'Christ of faith' is dissolved into an unhistorical myth, a philosophical idea, an existential, if his foundation, the historical Jesus, is taken away.

To sum up, a whole series of reasons may be recognized which caused the 'biography' of Jesus to be recounted in the apostolic age. It was not done for the joy of telling stories, or from historical curiosity, but from theological necessity. 'There would have been no tradition about Jesus, if there had been no preaching about Jesus' (Dibelius).

The 'Christ of Faith' and the Resurrection of Jesus from the Dead

The Gospel story shows how the crucifixion of Jesus could have come about at all. And that alone makes the cross historically understandable. Bultmann is therefore right in saying that this does not yet assign to the cross of Jesus any value in the line of salvation, at least not without further considerations. For this Cross, at first sight, stands there merely like the crosses of the two thieves, and like many other crosses that had been set up before. True, the New Testament gives us to understand that Jesus, while instructing his disciples, had already prepared them for a special insight into his death. This was done not merely in single sayings, such as Mark 10:45, and in the explanatory words at the Last Supper, but above all in the interpretation which he himself gave his ministry, when

he took the traditional concept of Son of Man and explained it in the light of the concept of the Servant of
Yahweh, as given in Isaias. Thus some understanding of
his death was undoubtedly imparted and prepared by the
historical Jesus. None the less, his disciples seem to have
been so shattered by his arrest and crucifixion that they
derived no hope from what they had been told (see Mt
26:56b; Mk 14:50; Lk 24:21; John 20:19). And yet we
find them proclaiming—and that no more than a few
weeks after the awful event of Golgotha—that the cross
of Jesus is the cross of Christ (to keep to the terms which
Bultmann uses). Somehow or other they must have learned
the significance of the Cross. How did this come about?
But to ask this question is meaningless, according to Bultmann. See his *Theology of the New Testament*, New York:
Scribners, p. 46: 'How the Easter faith was born in the
individual "disciples" has been obscured by legend in the
tradition. And the process itself is totally unimportant'.
To this we must say:

1) How the Easter faith of the disciples came about can
still be seen clearly enough. It was by the appearances of
the Risen Lord.

2) The apostolic preaching appears to have attributed
to this 'birth' of the Easter faith an importance of the
highest order, indeed, such as involves a total human
commitment (see in particular 1 Cor 15:5-8). In spite of
everything, Bultmann too is forced to give some explanation of how the Easter faith of the disciples could be born.
In *Kerygma und Mythos*, 1, 46, he writes: 'The Easter
event, looked on as the resurrection of Christ, is not
an historical event. The only tangible historical element
is the faith of the first disciples. How this arose the historian can make comprehensible, to a certain extent, by

reflecting on the previous personal attachment of the disciples to Jesus. For the historian, the Easter event comes down to their visionary experiences'. Elsewhere he says: 'When I dream of my friend, the dream-picture which I see for the moment is not of course the reflexion of a real condition. But I produce the dream about my friend only because I have met him in the sphere of reality. The dream comments, as it were, a really existent and present meeting. Similarly, the Resurrection "dream" of the disciples is also a reaction to what they have experienced along with Jesus Christ. The Resurrection-vision interprets the figure of Jesus as one who has conquered death'.

The fatal effort to reduce the origin of the Easter faith to visionary experiences of the disciples leads necessarily to making of the decisive foundations of Christianity a merely psychological process. In the long run, the Easter faith is reduced to the earlier experiences of the disciples, when they 'knew Christ according to the flesh' (see 2 Cor 5 : 16), and which Bultmann otherwise rejects so categorically as foundation of the faith. Further, in Bultmann's 'explanation' it is impossible to see why the disciples of Jesus, who was dead and buried, should have experienced him precisely as the one 'who has conquered death'—if he still continues to lie in his grave. Rengstorf suspects, and with justice, that the so-called 'Vision Theory', such as is constantly brought forward in recent times (since D. F. Strauss), already played a role in the early apostolic times in polemic against Christianity (see Mt 28 : 11 ff; Jn 20 : 15). This would be the best explanation of citing a formal list of witnesses for the apparitions, as is done in 1 Cor 15 : 5-8.

3) Without the real resurrection of Jesus from the dead, the (Easter) kerygma and the faith are 'empty', as St Paul

rightly concludes (1 Cor 15:14). When the Apostle puts it this way: 'If Christ be not risen, then is our preaching empty', then the logic of the phrase demands that for him the resurrection of Jesus from the dead is something *previous* to the kerygma, a presupposition of the kerygma. Without this presupposition, the kerygma would not have come about. Real, not visionary apparitions gave rise to the Easter faith of the disciples. The terminology in which the apparitions are recounted in the New Testament, especially the word 'appeared to' ('showed himself to'), leaves no doubt that the apparitions of the Risen Lord consisted of a real self-presentation of the Lord himself, something independent of the observers (Rengstorf).

We must note also that where St Paul has occasion to speak of his visions and revelations (2 Cor 12:1–7) he does not mention the apparition of Christ on the road to Damascus. He is therefore perfectly able to distinguish the experience before Damascus, which was the foundation of his apostolic office and of his preaching of Christ, and which in 1 Corinthians 15:8 he specifically puts on one level with the apparitions of the Risen Lord, from these private experiences of his own personal relationship to God, which he cites only unwillingly, when he has to put his opponents in their place. He knows then perfectly well that private revelations, visionary experiences and the like, are not the foundation of a revelation which could be put before the world as the message which brings salvation. Bultmann, to be sure, in spite of Galatians 1:12, does not derive St Paul's conversion from the Damascus experience, but from the 'Word' which confronted him in the kerygma of the Christian community—though there is not a word about this in the New Testament. He says (*Theology of the N.T.*, p. 184), 'He . . . was won to the Christian faith by the kerygma of the Hellenistic community'. But he does not explain how a community could have been formed before ever there was any kerygma.

The event of the resurrection of Jesus from the dead can indeed not be 'proved' by historical methods, but it cannot be gainsaid that in the New Testament real apparitions of the Risen Lord are described, and that in the Easter message of the New Testament the resurrection of Jesus is understood as the real resurrection of a man from physical death. The meeting of the Apostles with the Risen Lord was for them a renewal of meetings with the historical Jesus (see especially Jn 20: 27; Lk 24: 39). In the light of this new meeting, the history of Jesus, his total activity in deed and in word, becomes for the first time fully transparent: 'the unveiled reality of Jesus Christ is revealed to the witnesses as testimony' (Schlier).

In the light of the Easter event, the Christology which was contained in the claims of the historical Jesus is now unfolded. Titles of dignity and concepts which were already at hand in the biblical tradition and in the philosophical and religious culture of the surrounding world were used at times to develop that Christology. In the kerygma, the 'Jesus of history' becomes the 'Christ of faith', but in the form of a judgment of identity: Jesus = the Christ; Jesus = the Lord. These judgments leave no discontinuity between the 'two'. The 'Christ of faith' is only a consequence of the Easter event, at least according to the way the New Testament understands things. Easter, according to the New Testament, is no mere 'existential', no mere mental framework.

In the light of the Easter event the whole life of Jesus is now given a further interpretation and elevated into the kerygma. The 'biographies' of Jesus are written. These we have in the canonical Gospels, where now history and message form such a mysterious and inextricable inter-weaving. Hence it is that in the Gospels and the whole New Testament we have indeed historical documents, but such documents as bear witness to events which are seen *in the light of faith,* and therefore represent a certain *interpretation* of historical events. Therefore, between us and the historical Jesus there has been inserted an inter-pretative, competent voice, which says to us: So and in no other wise is the life of Jesus to be understood. Whether we will or no, we can no longer reach the historical Jesus except by the medium of this intervening voice. And this leads to a new question.

The Role and Rank of the Intermediaries
(The Bearers of Tradition)

The Gospels are explanations of the history of Jesus, explanations behind which the *apostolic* interpretation of the life of Jesus seems to lie. Is this interpretation the only correct and legitimate one? Is it the norm for our own understanding of Jesus?

It is certain, first of all, that the life of Jesus can be expounded otherwise than is done in the Gospels and the New Testament in general. The life of Jesus is not 'un-ambiguous' and even in the days of the historical Jesus was obviously not 'unambiguous'. The biography of Jesus, as we have it in the Gospels, still makes that clear. Here are some examples. We see from Mark 6: 14–16; 8: 27 f that Jesus' contemporaries were by no means in agreement in their verdict upon him. For some he is the Baptist risen again, for others Elias returned to life, while others again said, 'He is a prophet like one of the prophets' (6: 15).

The narrower circle of disciples, however, seem to have seen in Jesus the Messiah. Peter, in the name of all, makes the profession of faith, 'Thou art the Messiah' (8:29). Thus, when Jesus initiates the circle of disciples into the mystery of his Passion, Peter still revolts against it with all his energy (see 8:32; Mt 16:22). Apparently the mystery of the Passion did not fit into his picture of the Messiah. He has certainly misinterpreted Jesus' previous work, drawn false conclusions from it, linked other expectations to it, like the followers of Jesus who, according to Luke 19:11, thought that because he was near to Jerusalem 'the Kingdom of God would soon appear'. They therefore misunderstood his journey to Jerusalem and attached false hopes to it. And how does the people understand the entry into Jerusalem? In the very same way, it would appear. After the miraculous multiplication of bread by the lakeside, Jesus had to withdraw from the people, according to John 6:15, because they had misunderstood his 'sign'. They wanted to acclaim him as (messianic) King!

Jesus' messianic activity was therefore open to misunderstanding, and was misunderstood, even in the narrowest circle of his disciples. His own interpretation of the concept of Son of Man, in the light of Isaias' proclamation of the Servant of the Lord, remained unintelligible, because it did not conform to the Jewish notion of the Messiah. And finally, it appeared that he died 'without having redeemed Israel' (see Mk 15:32; Lk 24:21). Jesus' friendly contacts with tax-gatherers and sinners were not merely misunderstood, they were sharply criticized (see Mk 2:15 f; Lk 5:29 f; 7:39; 15:1; 19:7).

All these observations give us to understand that the life of Jesus urgently needed an explanation, in which Jesus' interpretation of himself would be taken up and carried

on. Have we this in the 'canonical' Gospels? This question
had to be decided, because besides the apostolic explanation preserved in these Gospels, the life of Jesus soon
began to receive new and quite different explanations, the
record of which has been preserved for us in the scanty
remains of the *apocryphal Gospels*. This state of affairs
shows, however, that some people were by no means ready
to accept the explanation of the life of Jesus which was
given in the Gospels later to be declared canonical. To go
more closely into the reasons for this might be interesting,
but would take us outside the framework of the present
study. The apocryphal tradition arose, it would seem, for
many reasons, one of which was criticism of the canonical.
No doubt the canonical tradition had a vital interest in
the historical Jesus, as we have seen. But this interest is
fundamentally different from the interest of the Apoc-
rypha, which was inspired by a crude curiosity and the
search for special mysteries in the Life of Jesus. Here
legend and myth took possession of the figure of Christ.

The remains of the apocryphal gospel-writing show
clearly that the life of Jesus could be given a commentary
other than that of the four 'canonical' Gospels. The Church
however decided in favour of these four alone. Why?
Certainly because the 'canonical' tradition and interpretation of the life of Jesus seemed to it the only correct one.
But why did the Church think so? The answer to this
question can only be: Because clearly the interpretation
of the history of Jesus given in the canonical Gospels
seemed to be the apostolic one. Thereby this is declared
to be the only authoritative and legitimate interpretation.
At the same time, the Church recognized two Gospels as
canonical which from the start were attributed to authors
who were not Apostles. Thereby the Church declared that

in them was contained true apostolic tradition about Jesus and hence therein the history of Jesus is correctly interpreted. Meanwhile, form-critical work has confirmed the fact that the Gospels of St Mark and St Luke also presuppose the 'Gospel before the Gospels', and that they have developed it further. Of course, the apocryphal gospels also worked with the 'canonical' tradition which lay before them, but they did so in a way completely different from that of St Mark and St Luke, as a brief comparison is enough to show.

In this connexion, we may be allowed to make some brief remarks about what is called form-criticism of the Gospels. Many Catholic theologians, when they hear of form-criticism, think at once of the term 'Community theology', which is in fact open to misunderstanding. They think therefore of form-criticism as if it attributed to the imaginary womb of the community a creative initiative and power in the production of the kerygma, which it exercised of itself. Form-criticism has further fallen into disfavour with many because its founders, especially M. Dibelius, took to categories which derive from modern history of literature, when naming the 'forms' of tradition. Dibelius used such names as 'Legend' and 'Novelle', which also claimed to give a judgment of historical value about individual traditions.

If this were its only meaning, the work of form-criticism would indeed have to be rejected. But if, on the contrary, our knowledge of form-criticism takes this form: the *Sitz im Leben*, the social setting, of the Christian community was a contributing factor to the *forms* in which the apostolic kerygma and the traditions about the life of Jesus were developed—Catholic theology has nothing against it. Above all, however, it is the permanent merit of form-

criticism, for which all must be grateful, that it demonstrated that the Gospels did not begin at the writers' desks
but represent a collective effort, into which has been
adopted the previous tradition about Jesus, 'the Gospel
before the Gospels' transmitted by the apostolic Church
and edited by the Evangelists. Thereby form-criticism has
proved that the principle of tradition is a biblical principle. It enables us precisely 'to recognize that the beginnings of the history of Jesus do not lie in the mythical, but
have their basis in real events' (Dibelius).

The decision of the Church in favour of the canonical
gospels obviously started from the conviction that the
Apostle is the only legitimate interpreter of the life of
Jesus. He is the normative 'intermediary'. Does this view
square with the New Testament conception of the Apostle?

The Greek term, *apostolos,* corresponds to the Hebrew
shaliach. The *shaliach* is the plenipotentiary envoy of the
one who has sent him. Now, the New Testament uses the
concept 'Apostle' in this sense too, but in addition makes
some important distinctions. In the New Testament the
term 'Apostle' is found as the designation of the group
who are otherwise called 'the Twelve'. But it is also used
to designate the envoys of various communities and wandering missionaries (e.g. Phil 2:25; Acts 8:14, 18 etc;
1 Cor 9:5; Rom 16:7). But in none of these latter texts
is it said that these 'Apostles' were 'Apostles of Jesus Christ'
(Lohse). The expression with the attribute in the genitive
is first found in 1 Thessalonians 2:7. From Galatians 1:1
we may conclude that it indicates an Apostle with special
qualifications, who is to be distinguished from the envoys
of the communities and the wandering missionaries. He
is the Apostle who has received his mission and his task
directly from the Lord himself. This qualification is obvi-

15

ously attributed by St Paul (Gal 1 : 17) to those 'who were Apostles before him' (see also 2 : 9). This new understanding of the office of the Apostle had as a consequence 'that the concept of Apostle received an absolutely fixed meaning, and was restricted to the group of the Twelve and to St Paul. Only these are Apostles of Jesus Christ in the true sense' (Lohse). The 'Apostle of Jesus Christ' is therefore one who can attribute his mission and his task directly to Jesus himself (see also Mt 28 : 16-20).

In the New Testament understanding of 'Apostle' in this special sense, another element must be noted which also is lacking in the late Jewish concept of the *shaliach*, and which is of particular importance for our theme. According to Acts 1 : 21, St Peter lays down as a condition for the election of a substitute for Judas: 'So one of those who have been with us, during all the time that the Lord Jesus went in and out among us, beginning from the baptism of John until the day when he was taken up from us, one of these must become with us a witness to his resurrection'. Membership in the College of the Twelve is, according to this statement, open only to a witness of the life of Jesus, and not just until the crucifixion, but until his ascension into heaven. He must therefore also be a witness of the apparitions of the Risen Lord. We may compare further Acts 10 : 39-41; 13 : 31; 5 : 32, in which the events to be attested also include at least the crucifixion. The Lucan concept of Apostle in the strict sense therefore includes the fact that he is a witness for the historical life of Jesus, including his apparitions after the resurrection. Only 'those who from the beginning were eye-witnesses' seem to be the guarantors of authentic 'tradition' about Jesus (see Lk 1 : 2). No doubt this conception of St Luke expresses the tendency to identify the chief factor of historical 'certainty' (see Lk 1:4) with regard to the Church tradition about Jesus: The accounts of Jesus of Nazareth go back to eye-witnesses.

The principle that the Apostle must be an eye-witness of the historical life of Jesus is however not confined to St Luke, but is found also in Mark 3:14. Jesus 'made Twelve, that they might be with him, and to send them out, to proclaim ...' The word 'proclaim', used without an object, indicates—at least to the Evangelists—not merely the preliminary mission of the Twelve in Galilee (see Mk 6:7-13), but also their later preaching activity after Pentecost. Daily intercourse with Jesus forms the foundation of their later preaching. There they learn to know the interpretation which Jesus himself gave to his ministry.

The principle of apostolic eye-witnessing is likewise Johannine, see John 15:27: 'And you also bear witness, because you have been with me from the beginning'. The present tense of 'witness' ascribes to the disciples the role which they shall play. You are (to be) witnesses, 'because you are with me from the beginning' (Bultmann). Here the quality of eye-witness is linked to an interest which is very dear to St John elsewhere. The attested tradition must go back to the 'Beginning', meaning here the 'Beginning' of the public life of Jesus. The quality of eye-witness is also emphasized very strongly by St John in other places (19:35; 1 Jn 1:2; 4:14). (See also 1 John 1:1; 2:7; 24; 3:11.) The eye-witness is the founder and bearer of true and valid tradition! The eye-witness 'keeps' the 'word' which Jesus spoke while he was with them (Jn 14:24 f).

The concepts of witness, testimony and giving testimony, come from the language of the law-courts. Witnesses are summoned before the publicity of the courts, in order to testify to actual facts which they themselves have experienced. If the Apostles, in the mind of the New Testament, are designated as witnesses of the historical life of Jesus, the logic of the concept demands that they bear witness for historical facts. Special value, according to the indications furnished by the Acts of the Apostles, is given to their testimony to the apparitions and thereby to the resurrection of Jesus from the dead. For in some places, the appeal to the eye-witnesses is restricted to the fact of the resurrection of Jesus, which was manifested in the apparitions which the eye-witnesses attest. Thus the summary narratives of Acts 2:32; 3:15; 4:33.

Notable also is the fact that in all these texts from the Acts the plural is used: 'we are witnesses'. Matthias too is to become a witness 'along with us'. This may stem partly from the Old Testament and Jewish idea that an assertion is valid only when it has at least two witnesses (see Dt 19:15; Jos 8:17). It also derives from the view that the tradition presented by the apostolic preaching is unanimous and without contradictions. A 'different' historical Jesus is not attested.

According to 2 Corinthians 11:4, there is no other Jesus than he who is attested by the apostolic preaching. But St Paul too thinks of apostolic eye-witness with regard to the risen Jesus. See 1 Corinthians 15:15, 'If God has not really raised up Jesus from the dead, then we shall be found to be false witnesses for God, because we have testified against God that he has raised up Christ'. St Paul too uses the plural, which is certainly not a 'rhetorical' one here, but looks back at the series of witnesses named in 15:5-8, at least at the Twelve. Clearly, with regard to the resurrection of Jesus, the eye-witness is the decisive factor, more important even than with regard to the previous life of Jesus. Why?

St Paul gives the reason with all desirable clarity: because otherwise our (Easter) kerygma would be 'empty' (15: 14). Consequently, it would be meaningless to proclaim and attest the rest of the life of Jesus. The telling of the life of Jesus attains the rank of kerygmatic preaching, and only becomes fully intelligible, through the great event, his rising from the dead. By it alone Jesus becomes perfectly recognizable as the decisive eschatological event and by it alone does he become the subject of preaching. There is still, on the other hand, in the concept of apostolate as given in the Gospels and the Acts, a strong emphasis on the quality of eye-witness with regard to the public life of Jesus which preceded the resurrection. Why is this? Apparently, because it is looked on as containing a guarantee for the continuity of the Christ of faith and the historical Jesus. The 'Christ of faith' proclaimed by the Apostles is none other than he 'with whom they were together from the beginning'.

Granted then that 'Apostle' in the strict sense means a witness for the historical Jesus, the question arises whether St Paul can be a 'witness' for Jesus in the sense in which St Luke uses the word. St Paul may indeed have known the historical Jesus (see 2 Cor 5: 16), still it is primarily the living Lord, who has conquered death, that has significance for him. This is he whom he has 'seen' (1 Cor 9: 1; 15: 8), and this gives him consciousness of being one of the number of the Apostles of Jesus Christ: 'Am I not an Apostle? Have I not seen our Lord Jesus?' (See also Gal 1: 15 f.) St Paul does not therefore come forward as a witness for the earthly Jesus as do the Twelve, but as witness for the resurrection (see 1 Cor 15: 8, 15 and our remarks above). However, Acts 1: 21 also emphasizes that Matthias is to be 'witness of his resurrection'. Further, as remarked above, in three further places of Acts St Luke restricts the function of witness to the apparitions of the Risen Lord. The important thing therefore, even for St Luke, in the concept of the Apostle as witness, is that they have seen the Risen Lord like St Paul. Only on this basis could any tradition at all have been created about the life of Jesus. We must also remember that St Paul presupposes the historical Jesus, who is no more and no less present in the epistles than in the rest of the New Testament. Bultmann says: 'The historical person of Jesus is what first makes Paul's preaching a Gospel'. The Apostle names very important data from the life of Jesus, as for instance his descent from David (Rom 1 : 3). And when it is called for, the Apostle has recourse to the 'Word' of Jesus which is present in the 'tradition'.

The peculiar nature of the Gospel 'biography' of Jesus allows us however to recognize that the apostolic witness for the life of Jesus had a very special quality. The Apostle does not produce a film with a sound-track; he has no tape recordings to play back; rather, he interprets at once the life of Jesus. But is that compatible with his role of 'Apostle' and 'witness'? 'The *shaliach* had to follow out his instructions strictly in all his tasks, and was not allowed to go a step beyond them' (Lohse). The 'Apostle of Jesus Christ' however did not understand himself to be bound by such limitations: his understanding of his apostolic task went far beyond the mind of the *shaliach*.

One could of course point to the fact that the writers of the Synoptic stories were naïve enough to think that their narratives gave only the 'history' of Jesus. Such a view would overlook the fact that from the very start even the Synoptic writers were not at all interested in writing a biography of Jesus in the strictly historical sense. From the

start, each of them drew up his story of Jesus 'kerygmati-
cally', from certain Christological stand-points, which influenced even the formal structure of the single pericopes.
Their sketch of the life of Jesus is dominated for instance
by their effort to point it towards a goal, a principle which
is already to be found in Jesus' own self-explanation, as
for instance in the 'redemption' saying (Mk 10:45).

It is also ruled by a selective principle, which only brings
to memory what is necessary to reach their kerygmatic ends.
This holds good even for the 'historian' of the Synoptics,
St Luke, for he does not aim at completeness but at
'certainty' (1:4), by which he means, apparently, not primarily the reliability of the facts but of those 'traditions'
(1:2) which have been put forward during instruction in
the faith. So 1:4: 'that you may be able to convince yourself of the reliability of the words about which you have
been instructed'. The process of giving testimony seems to
have been guided by such principles *from the start*, as the
outlines of the apostolic preaching of salvation in the Acts
still allow us to see.

Even in the book of the New Testament in which the
terminology of 'witnessing' plays the greatest part, the
Gospel of St John, the concept of 'witness' contains more
than the element of merely 'objective' reporting—if there
ever is such a thing. To 'bear witness' here means rather
an inspired act of preaching and confessing. The Spirit of
truth, whom Jesus will send from the Father, will give
testimony to him, 'and you too bear witness' (Jn 15:26 f).
The Apostles' testimony to Christ will be made one with
the Spirit's testimony to Christ. Indeed, the Spirit of truth
will be with the disciples and remain with them (14:17 b),
'teaching them all things' and 'bringing all things to mind'
that Jesus has said to them (14:26), and 'leading them unto

all truth' (16:13). Thus, according to the preaching of St John, the Spirit along with the apostolic witnesses of the life of Jesus is the guarantee of the integrity of the tradition about Jesus. Indeed, there is more: He it is who keeps alive the 'memory' of Jesus and 'leads' to a full understanding of Jesus and of his message.

But it must be clearly grasped that the work of the Spirit may not be isolated from the revelation given by Jesus. For it is the glorified Lord himself who sends him (Jn 15:26; 16:8; see also 14:16, 26; 16:7; Mk 1:8; Lk 24:49; Acts 2:33). And the function of the Spirit is not to make additions, it is that of 'guidance' (Jn 16:13), that is, the function of disclosing and explaining the truth and the mystery of *Jesus* (see Jn 14:26; 15:26; 16:14). Thus it is only the Spirit that equips the witnesses fully for their task of giving testimony. In the testimony of the apostolic witnesses we hear at the same time the Spirit of God, giving inspiration and interpretation, and he is indissolubly united to the glorified Lord.

The Acts of the Apostles sees things in the same way. For according to its presentation of events, the public testimony of the witnesses only begins after the mission of the Spirit at Pentecost, to receive whom 'the sacred number of twelve Apostles has been restored' (Haenchen), by the election of Matthias. In the sermon of St Peter (5:32) 'we . . . and the Holy Spirit' are named in one breath as 'witnesses of these events'. According to Luke 24:44-49, also, the risen Lord first reminds the Apostles of his former words about the divine necessity (Greek : *deî*) of the Scriptures being fulfilled in him, then opens their previously closed minds (see Lk 9:45; 18:34) to a truly 'Christological' understanding of the Scriptures, and finally refers to the preaching of salvation to all the nations 'beginning from Jerusalem', which was already demanded by the Scriptures. The Apostles are 'witnesses to this' (24 : 48), that is, ready for the mission to the gentiles, 'because having experienced it at first hand, they can give testimony to the Passion and Resurrection of Jesus; likewise because they have grasped in faith the meaning of Jesus, and for this reason too can "bear witness" to it' (Strathmann). But they must first remain in the city, 'till you are given power from on high' (Acts 1 : 8). Rengstorf notes that the concept of the apostolic witness also includes the fact that he is 'also interpreter of the Scriptures'. The Apostle takes up in his testimony Jesus' 'Christological' interpretation, and develops it further. Hence the oldest kerygma is already linked with interpretation of Scripture.

According to the New Testament therefore, the Apostles are enabled to 'bear witness' by a two-fold quality. They have been 'together with' Jesus before and after his resurrection (see for the latter especially Acts 10 : 41). And they have the 'helper' whom the glorified Lord sends them. As the New Testament understands it, then, the witness of the Apostles means to make an assertion in public about past events, and likewise, to understand these assertions thoroughly and to seek to win men for what they have attested.

Since the Spirit of God is indissolubly united to the glorified Lord himself, we may fully accept the thesis put forward by O. Cullmann, 'that the Christ who has been exalted to the right hand of God is the bearer of tradition behind the Apostles, who transmit his words and deeds'. This 'behind the Apostles' must of course be in no wise weakened or suppressed. The voice of the glorified Lord is never otherwise present than 'behind the Apostles' and, fundamental theology would add, their successors. Hence the question of 'certainty about Jesus of Nazareth' can never be answered in this direction: 'The way to absolute certainty about Jesus of Nazareth as a man in history, and about the events of his life leads therefore exclusively (!) through the Christ himself present to-day, who "in, with and under" the word, identifies himself with the Jesus of the New Testament' (Engelland). For 'the word', meaning presumably the word of Sacred Scripture brought forward in the preaching, is as a matter of fact not any longer just the immediate word of Jesus, but the word of Jesus attested by the Apostles, which I can reach only in historical documents. Certainly, the word remains dead if it does not affect my life, if I do not let myself be reached by God with it. But even if it touches me, I am still far from knowing that it is the word of Jesus of Nazareth, so long as I do not accept it as such from the Apostles, whose witness is preserved in the New Testament, unless I betake myself into some strange region of mysticism. The certainty that Jesus is my Lord is given to me by the preaching of the word by those that were 'sent' (see Rom 10: 14, 15).

St Paul, in Romans 10: 8–18, gives a precise set of steps from the 'word' (of Christ) to the faith of the hearers of it. The word of Christ is 'near', not immediately so from his lips, but only through the medium of the 'preachers'. And then he asks (in verse 15) 'but how shall they preach, if they have not been sent?' The whole section is concerned on the one hand with the unbelief of Israel, and on the other hand with the confessing of Jesus, his resurrection from the dead, the invocation of his name, the Gospel and the word of Christ. Thus there can be no doubt that St Paul is speaking of his own (bitter) experience and that of the other missionaries who sought to convert the Jews.

St Paul therefore understands his own apostolic task and that of his fellow-Apostles in the sense that he is a necessary 'intermediate link' in the chain: word of Christ—preaching—faith. The Apostle is inserted in between, and without him there could be no preaching at all. Without the voice of the Apostle in between, the word of Christ would not be present at all or perceptible, and in consequence there would be no such thing as faith in '*Jesus as the Lord*' (see Rom 10:9). So too Matthew 28:20: 'teach them to observe all that I have commanded you' and the Epistle to the Hebrews 2:3: salvation 'took its start in the preaching *by the Lord*, and was confirmed unto us by *those who heard it*'. Between the Lord and ourselves comes the intermediate voice of the witnesses who heard him themselves!

Thus an analysis of the New Testament concept of Apostle (witness) confirms what we had already learned in another way: that we reach the historical Jesus only through the medium of the apostolic preaching. The apostolic witness has been inserted between the historical Jesus and the Christ of faith as a necessary, unavoidable, 'intermediate voice'. Since this witness was hearer and eye-witness of the historical Jesus, including the risen Jesus; since in his explanation of the history of Jesus he continues Jesus' self-explanation; and since in this he is guided by the 'Spirit of truth', his fellow-witness, sent by the glorified Lord himself, the interpretation of the history of Jesus given in the New Testament is the only legitimate and normative one. Thus, as the New Testament understands it, the apostolic witnesses are the ultimate guarantee of the oneness and continuity of the Christ of faith and the historical Jesus.

Results and Consequences

Are we finally back to the stand-point of Kähler? We have recognized, like Kähler, the unity of the historical Jesus and the Christ of faith in the apostolic preaching contained in the New Testament. But all the same, the differences between our solution and that of Kähler are fundamental. Kähler gave his lecture the title: 'The So-called Historical Jesus and the Biblical Christ of Faith'. The results of our enquiries forbid us to formulate the subject in this manner, and here the difference begins to show itself. The 'so-called' historical Jesus of Kähler had indeed a special background, namely, the nineteenth century's research into the life of Jesus, and Kähler was right in rejecting the 'historical Jesus' it produced. But Kähler's uncritical retreat to the 'Biblical Christ' cannot be the right way. For the historical Jesus is in fact present in the Gospels, and can therefore be reached there, not merely 'in faith', but also *by the route of historical research*, which Kähler held to be fruitless. The apostolic preaching is no doubt convinced of the unity of this historical Jesus with the 'Christ of faith' which it preached, but it is convinced entirely on the basis of the history of Jesus and his historical claims. The Apostles bear witness not to the 'Christ of faith' but to the historical Jesus. All they do in their preaching is to bring the nature and the claims of the historical Jesus into their true light, so that they appear in their full force.

If that is so, then historical questions continue to have a place, and indeed a necessary one, in study of the Gospels. That means that questions as to authenticity, say with regard to the sayings of Jesus or the chronology and topography of his life, are not to be shelved on principle, but can be discussed quite fruitfully, so long as one keeps in mind the limits of the attainable. It is true that a 'Life of Our Lord' can no longer be attempted in the way that was done formerly, since the Gospels do not intend to offer a continuous biography in the ordinary historical sense. And yet the subject of the Gospels is the historical life of Jesus, or better, the historical Jesus; and hence the effort to present his life by means of historical methods is quite in order, as long as this effort remains conscious of the limits set to it by the peculiar nature of the Gospel story of Jesus itself.

The New Testament itself testifies to the fact that the apostolic hearers and eye-witnesses of the life of Jesus are not merely vehicles of tradition but are, while performing this function, inspired witnesses. From this it follows, though not from this alone, that the tradition of the words and deeds of Jesus was a living process, as may also be seen from a careful study of the Gospels. Because in fact the 'eye-witnesses and servants of the word' (Lk 1:2) applied the tradition about Jesus to the concrete needs and situations of the Christian communities, the tradition took on various forms in the Synoptics, for instance, so that there is hardly any 'triple tradition' where there is not a difference in at least *one* word. We have only to think of the words of the institution of the Eucharist. In the process of the Gospel tradition a number of stages must be distinguished: a) the historical situation in the life of Jesus; b) the original apostolic account of the words and deeds of Jesus; c) the transmission of these accounts, interpreted and applied to the various mission communities; d) efforts at fixing the matter of tradition in writing (see Lk 1:1); e) the definitive editing of the apostolic tradition of the Church by the evangelists.

This process of transformation which the tradition underwent at the hands of the 'intermediaries' has obviously been taken to its furthest stage in the fourth Gospel. These are undeniable facts, which will not disturb those who know that the rule of faith is the living voice of the teaching Church. The misery of the Protestant discussion of the historical Jesus has as one of its causes, undoubtedly, that Protestant theology with its different conception of the Church has no correct approach to the theological status of the apostolic 'intermediate voice'. Hence it wavers constantly between a purely 'kerygmatic' theology and historical criticism, without finding a convincing, living synthesis. The tradition about Jesus is not to be separated from the voice which transmits it!

W. G. Kümmel says that 'no general assertion of the historical reliability of the Gospel tradition can be upheld', for instance, 'on the ground that the historical Jesus is attested by the Apostles who were guided by the Holy Spirit'. But the *transmission* is a fact whose significance for the formation of the tradition must be investigated historically and theologically. When the role of the 'intermediate voice' has been noted and emphasized, critical investigation of the Gospel tradition with regard to the sayings of Jesus, for instance, does not become by any means superfluous. Only, all factors must be taken into account.

The Church was from the beginning the actual setting of the tradition about Jesus. This is important, from the point of view of fundamental theology (apologetics) for the quest of the historical Jesus. The problem of 'exegesis and dogmatics', to which this volume of essays by various authors is directed, can only be correctly seen and solved, with regard to the question of 'Historical Jesus, the Christ

of faith', when the theological status of the apostolic intermediaries is also sufficiently weighed. This is of course to
be done with constant reference to the historical question
of the consciousness which Jesus had of himself, a question
which may not be eliminated if theology is to remain a
science.

Karl
Rahner, S.J.

DOGMATIC CONSIDERATIONS ON KNOWLEDGE AND CONSCIOUSNESS IN CHRIST

The theme of this brief and modest conference consists in some dogmatic considerations on how Christ as man knew himself, and his knowledge in general. The problem which it sets up needs no long introduction, as it is treated in all older and newer literature on Christology. The theological tradition attributes to Jesus as man a knowledge which embraces and penetrates everything past, present and future in finite reality, at least in so far as it has to do with his salvific mission. Thus for instance the encyclical *Mystici Corporis* (1943) ascribes to Jesus an express knowledge of all men in all ages. Theological tradition further attributes to Jesus the direct vision of God from the first moment of his existence, a vision such as that which the blessed in heaven have in the final state of glory.

Such assertions, at first hearing, seem to savour almost of mythology. They seem to deny that the Lord was really a human being, subject to the growth and change of human life. They seem at first sight to come into hopeless conflict with the data of Sacred Scripture, which speaks of a de-

16

veloping consciousness in Jesus (Lk 2:52), of a Lord who himself professes ignorance of decisive matters definitely part of his mission (Mt 24:36; Mk 13:32). He is shown as a man bearing the stamp of his times, as modern research into ancient religion and culture demonstrates clearly, and with ever-increasing precision. We almost have the impression that the only original thing about him was his own personality, and the unique manner in which the influences of his milieu were concentrated in him—though every single human being is in his own way a unique sounding-board for his milieu.

The standard manuals of dogmatics have their solution. We are to distinguish an 'infused' knowledge from an 'acquired' knowledge, which is not excluded by the former. We are to remember the 'condescension' of the Lord in freely and deliberately adapting himself to his surroundings. We are to distinguish direct from indirect knowledge. But all this sounds artificial and improbable. Indeed, we even have the impression that all that is aimed at is merely verbal reconciliation between what history and dogma have to say about the self-consciousness of Jesus.

The question is therefore in the category of those which undeniably cause a certain strain between exegetes and dogmatic theologians. This strain is mostly 'relieved' by a sort of pretence between them that the other does not exist. Thus O. Karrer can say in his *Neues Testament*, that 'Even the Son during his earthly pilgrimage had not yet the blessed vision of God as at the right hand of the Father'. Modern exegetes, like J. Schmid, do not deal with the dogmatic question which arises from these texts. A public breach is avoided simply because formulas are sought which prevent one discipline from coming into express contradiction with the views of the other. But justice is not thereby done to the real situation.

In recent literature, however, the discussion has taken a turn which shows that an honest endeavour to bring both sides together and to find new and more objective solutions is not always lacking. The book of my colleague, E. Gutwenger on the consciousness and knowledge of Christ may be consulted as a good example, which gives also a survey of previous literature on the subject (Innsbruck, 1960). And a conference devoted to Christology by French theologians meeting at the Dominican house at Eveu took as its main theme the subject we are now discussing. We may at least refer in passing to the fact that in recent years dogmatic theologians have been engaged in discussing the problem of the 'I' of Christ (see for instance P. Galtier, *L'Unité du Christ : Etre-Personne-Conscience*, Paris 1939). These discussions have chiefly concerned the question of his consciousness, his creaturely self-consciousness, which has been treated from various dogmatic stand-points: that of post-Chalcedon theology, of the original theology of Chalcedon, or of the *Assumptus Homo* theology or the so-called Baslist theology (see *Revue Thomiste*, 1950, 1951). The articles of R. Haubst, in *Theologische Revue*, Münster, 1956 and in the *Trierer Theologische Zeitschrift*, 1957, give a good survey of the debate, which dispenses us from entering here upon this field of modern theological disputation.

We may emphasize here that the considerations which follow are of a purely dogmatic nature. We have neither the intention nor the competence to do an exegetical study. All we aim at is to put before the exegete a dogmatic view of the self-consciousness of Jesus and of his knowledge which will enable him to concede more easily than before that it is compatible with the results of his historical research. We say, 'compatible'. More is not in place. The exegete is not asked to use his historical method, or a biblical theology based immediately on the texts, to reach by himself the assertions of dogmatic theology with regard to the consciousness and knowledge of Jesus. No doubt such assertions are ultimately based on what Jesus himself said about his own person. The doctrine of the 'Hypostatic Union' of the Word with a human nature in Jesus Christ derives in the long run from such words of Jesus, at least as they were seen in the light of Easter. It has therefore a basis in the New Testament, and this doctrine of the Hypostatic Union is the foundation of the dogmatic assertions about the consciousness and knowledge of Jesus. But this of itself is enough to make it clear that such assertions do not come within the immediate scope of the exegete's work.

If, then, we make dogmatic assertions about the consciousness and knowledge of Jesus, all we aim at from the start is to propound a view which is tolerable in the light of its results. We hope to do this as well as possible, but no more. To go beyond this is neither necessary nor possible. In all this, we do not touch the question whether New Testament theology, in so far as it differs from the utterances of the historical Jesus about his own person, already contains assertions about the consciousness and knowledge of Jesus which involve an immediate vision of God.

After these introductory remarks, let us try to come to the heart of our question as quickly and immediately as possible, by denying ourselves reminiscences from the history of dogma and theology. In one short hour, we could not present such reminiscences with the exactness necessary. What we shall say makes no claim at all to be obligatory theological doctrine. It means only to be a tolerable theological view, which does not contradict the official declarations of the Church on the subject, which seems to be meaningful because it seems to be deducible from solid dogmatic positions, which can be reconciled, without forcing things, with the historical results of research into the life of Jesus. The positive solution which we offer makes no change in the official declarations of the Church on this question, even with regard to those which have not an absolutely binding force, that is, are not solemn definitions. Hence we can spare ourselves the trouble of asking what is the exact theological note or qualification of this traditional doctrine in the declarations of the teaching office of the Church.

The first thing to say in preparation for the discussion proper is this: Knowledge is a structure of many levels, so that with regard to these different dimensions of consciousness and knowledge, something may very well be both known and unknown. This means that one has the impression that in the discussion about the knowledge of Christ, theologians start from the silent assumption that the conscious intellect of man is indeed that famous *tabula rasa,* a blank space, on which something is inscribed or not, and so the question of its being written on or not can only be answered by a simple yes or no.

But things are in fact otherwise. Human consciousness is a space of endlessly multiple dimensions. Consciousness can be fully reflective or merely marginal. Something can be present to consciousness and expressly attended to. There is an objective conceptual consciousness, and also a transcendental knowledge, unreflective, situated at the subjective pole of the consciousness. There is a knowledge which is definite and composed of judgments and there is knowledge admitted or suppressed. There are psychical events in consciousness and their reflective interpretation. And finally, there is a knowledge which is not directed to an object of the formal horizon within which a definitely perceived object is set, and which is the conscious *a priori* condition, not in the nature of an object, of the object perceived *a posteriori* and the knowledge of the object itself. All this is really obvious, but is too little heeded in our question. Of course it is well known, in the discussion of our problem, that there are different kinds of knowledge, and distinctions are made between infused and acquired knowledge, and these concepts are again subject to sub-distinctions.

But these different kinds of knowledge are more or less expressly considered as different ways in which knowledge of objects can be acquired, and not precisely as different ways in which a reality can be known. They are looked on as the different ways in which the blank space of consciousness can be written on, not as the totally different ways in which a reality can be present in the many-dimensional space of consciousness. It cannot therefore be our task to draw up an empirical psychological or a transcendental table of such different manners of the presence of the object to the consciousness. The indications here given are intended merely to point to the fact of the manifold possibilities of the forms in which a reality can be an object of consciousness. They do not attempt to distinguish sharply one from another the different ways of such presence to consciousness, such consciousness, such knowing, such basic conditions and determinations.

Here we call attention to two things only. One, that among these forms of knowledge there is a knowledge, concerned with itself, which is *a priori* and not concentrated on an object, and which is a basic condition of existence for the spiritual subject. In it the subject is present to himself, and at the same time is aware of his transcendental relation to the totality of possible objects of knowledge and freedom. This basic condition is not knowledge of an object, and normally one is not concerned with it. Reflexion never grasps this basic condition adequately, even when it aims expressly at it. Reflective conceptual knowledge of it, where such exists, is not the thing itself but, once more, is something of which it is the vehicle, whence it never grasps adequately this original basic condition.

Further, reflexion on this basic condition need not necessarily succeed; it can perhaps even be impossible. Its successful accomplishment, which is asymptotic, can be dependent on the external data of external experience, which are given in historical contingence, and on conceptual material elsewhere derived, and its actual nature. To have some sort of idea of the meaning and correctness of the propositions just formulated—which ideally of course should be precisely and fully proved—we have only to consider that the spirituality, the transcendence, the freedom, the reference to absolute being which are given in each day-by-day act of the man who is concerned with any degree of indifference with his biological self-assertion. They are given not in the form of assertions or of known objects, but they are really present in consciousness. Indeed, being the primary data of consciousness they are of transcendental necessity and comprehensive significance as vehicles of knowledge. Still, they can only be grasped in the form of assertions and objects after the greatest effort, which called for a long history of spiritual development and brought with it the greatest possible variation in the history of terminology, as well as a varying success and the greatest difference of opinion in their interpretation.

The second preliminary remark consists in a criticism of the Greek ideal of man, in which knowledge is simply the absolute measure of man. This means that a Greek concept of man can consider a given piece of ignorance *only* as a falling short of the perfection to which man is ordained as to his end. Ignorance is simply something to be surpassed, no positive function can be attributed to it. That which is absent, in ignorance, is simply what is missing, but this absence is not regarded as the clearing of an open space for freedom and action, which can be more important than the simple presence of a given reality to the mind.

We men of the present day can no longer think so undialectically of knowing and not knowing. And for this we have objective reasons. We cannot here consider the positiveness of non-knowing, the *docta ignorantia*, in all its facets. But we may here call attention to one thing. It would surely be relatively easy for a philosophy of the person, of the freedom of the finite being, of history and of decision, to show that a risk is of the essence of the self-perfecting of the finite person in the historical freedom of decision. Risk is involved; coming out into the open is involved; committing oneself to what is not totally visible, the hidden origin and the veiled end—a certain manner of not-knowing is essential to the free act of man. And freedom always demands the wise evacuation of the area of freedom, its voluntarily accepted emptiness, as its own dark foothold, as the condition of its possibility. There is therefore undoubtedly an ignorance which, since it renders possible the accomplishment of the free act of the finite person while the drama of his history is still being played, is more perfect than a knowledge, in the act of the free will which would abolish the latter. Hence there is also a really positive will with regard to such ignorance. Actually, in the will to absolute transcendence directed to the infinite and incomprehensible Being in general, there is already a space for the unknown, which must always be accepted.

The nature of the spirit is to be directed towards the mystery, which is God, *quâ* mystery. All the clarity of the spirit is founded on its being referred to the eternal Incomprehensible as such. This is true even in the beatific vision, which does not mean the ending of the mystery, but the absolute nearness of this mystery as such, and the final blessed acceptance of it. It follows then once more from the final perfection of the spirit that one must be very prudent if one is tempted to qualify any degree of ignorance as pure negativity in the being of man. What, if anything, follows under certain circumstances from this consideration with regard to our specific subject can only be determined later.

We come now very rapidly to the real centre of our considerations. They are dogmatic in nature. We ask therefore: What reasons are there to oblige us to accept, along with the theology of the Catholic schools and the teaching office, that Jesus possessed already during his earthly life an immediate vision of God, such as is basis and kernel of the beatific vision of those who have attained their full end? When we put the matter so, we wish to indicate, by the very terms in which the question is couched, that one should not begin by saying 'beatific vision' (as I have already emphasized in my *Theological Investigations*, Baltimore, Md.: Helicon, Vol I, 149 ff).

First of all, it is a supposition too easily taken for

granted, that the immediate presence of God must always be the source of bliss. Why should the absolute nearness and immediacy to God—one can ask this without being a Scotist as regards the mode of bliss—since it is direct contact with the all-consuming justice and holiness of the incomprehensible God, be necessarily and always productive of blessedness? Further, is it certain that what is meant in theological tradition with regard to the consciousness of Jesus really wishes to assert a blessedness in his immediacy to God, beyond that state itself? And given the contents of the historical sources, which speak of Jesus' mortal terror and of his abandonment by God on the cross, can we, in all seriousness and without an artificial many-storeyed psychology, maintain that Jesus had such bliss as the blessed in heaven—and so make of him someone who is no longer really fulfilling his existence as 'pilgrim' authentically?

If one may answer these questions in the negative, the problem we are dealing with is simply this: what are the theological reasons that can be put forward which give us correct grounds for saying that Jesus possessed in his earthly life an immediate consciousness of God, a *visio immediata*, but that it was not *beata*, a beatific vision? What are the reasons which allow us not to qualify it as blessed? (We may note that the *beata* (*visio*) of Denzinger 2289, or the *beati* of Denzinger 2183 may be understood at once as a specificative qualification, and not as reduplicative. That Jesus on earth was not simply as blissful as the blessed in heaven can just not be denied. To assert the contrary would be an heretical denial of his sufferings, which were not just physiological.)

Once the question has been posed so precisely, we may make a preliminary observation before answering it. The

possible answers may be divided into two groups, of their
nature and according to the indications given by the history of theology. The first group of answers, which allow
naturally of many variations, ascribes such immediacy to
Jesus because and in so far as they start from the principle
that Jesus even on earth must be credited with all the
perfections which are not simply irreconcilable with his
earthly mission, especially if these perfections can be
proved or made probable further as helps and more or less
necessary presuppositions for his teaching authority. In
this group of answers therefore, the *visio immediata* is still
something superadded. It is not of the nature of things.
At the very most it is a perfection and a gift which follows
the Hypostatic Union by a sort of moral necessity, as for
example an infused knowledge is postulated for Jesus on
similar grounds. This set of answers to our question is
then more dependent on the appeal to the testimony of
Scripture and Tradition than is the second group, of
which we shall speak shortly.

An 'envoy of God', a *divinus legatus,* a prophet, is quite
thinkable without *visio immediata*; and the principle that
all perfections and privileges must be ascribed to Jesus
which are not incompatible with his mission (such as of
course freedom from suffering) finds itself faced with the
question of what the *visio immediata* implies. It is in
practice mostly considered as a 'blessed' vision, and the
question is whether the vision is incompatible with Jesus'
mission and way of life on earth. In view of the historical
data of the life of Jesus, the compatibility can be maintained only with many reserves and much obscurity. In
addition, it must be said that this group of answers lacks
the necessary support in tradition, especially when one
takes into account how unquestioningly the Greeks took

silent presuppositions into tradition, which are human, and not dogmatic.

If one appeals merely to the teaching office of the Church, the dogmatic theologian must be reminded that it is precisely his duty to show how and whence the *magisterium* of to-day has derived its doctrine. It receives of course no new revelations, but only preserves and expounds the apostolic tradition, so must itself have objective reasons for this its interpretation of the apostolic tradition. The recourse to the doctrine of the teaching office of the Church is therefore insufficient, especially as this doctrine up to the present has not been put forward with the obligatory character of a definition, and as regards its content can still be interpreted in essentially different manners. For this reason alone, the first group of answers (the extrinsicist theory, as we may call it) does not appear very commendable.

The second group of answers sees the *visio immediata* as an intrinsic element of the Hypostatic Union. It is simply given along with this and so cannot be renounced on any grounds. Hence an immediate testimony to it in tradition at all times is quite unnecessary, and it can be defined more exactly from the nature of the Hypostatic Union, which is for our considerations decisive. What can be said of the *visio immediata*, by virtue of the Hypostatic Union, must be asserted; and what is not derivable from the Hypostatic Union need not be maintained theologically, in so far as no sure and theologically binding complementary tradition can be cited—and probably there is no such tradition.

We must now explain more exactly what we mean, and since our time is so short, in the briefest possible speculative consideration, which will renounce any proofs from the history of theology. We start from the axiom of a Thomist theory of knowledge, according to which being and presence to oneself are mutually causative elements of the one reality, and hence any being is present to itself in the measure in which it has or is being. This means that the inner analogy and variability of being and potentiality stand in an absolutely simple and equal relation to the possibility of being present to self, of self-possession in knowledge, of consciousness. We cannot here develop more closely this axiom with regard to its sense or justification, but let us suppose it for once, and apply it to the reality of the Hypostatic Union.

The Hypostatic Union means the self-communication of the absolute being of God, as it subsists in the Word, to the human nature of Christ which is borne by it hypostatically. It is the highest thinkable, ontologically the highest actualization of a created reality which is absolutely possible, the highest form of being which exists at all outside God. The only thing comparable to it, at the very best, is the divine self-communication by means of uncreated grace in justification and glory, in so far as these come under the concept of a quasi-formal and not an efficient causality, since it is not a created reality but the uncreated being of God himself which is communicated with a creature. The Hypostatic Union is an ontological appropriation of a human nature by the person of the Word. But it is also (whether formally or consecutively need not be investigated here) a determination of the human reality by the person of the Word. It is therefore at least the actuation of the *potentia obedientialis* of the basic possibility of assumption, and so is something on the part of the creature, especially as the theology of the schools emphasizes that the Word does not change in the

Hypostatic Union, but that all that happens—and here there is the most radical event of all—takes place on the side of the creature.

According to the axiom of Thomist metaphysics of knowledge just laid down, this supreme ontological determination of the creaturely reality of Christ, which is God himself in his hypostatic quasi-formal causality, must necessarily be conscious of itself. For that which is ontologically higher can according to this axiom not be on a lower level of consciousness than that which is ontologically lesser. If there is therefore in this human reality a self-consciousness, then this ontological self-communication of God is also, indeed really and truly and above all, an element of the way in which the human subjectivity of Christ is present to itself. A purely ontic *Unio Hypostatica* is, in other words, a metaphysically impossible concept. The *visio immediata* is an inner element of the Hypostatic Union itself. And what has been said here is only an indication of what is here meant, and of the direction taken by the second group of answers to our opening question. We do not pretend that all this does not need a much more profound and exact explanation.

Nor do we mean to say that this recognition of the *visio immediata* as an inner element of the Hypostatic Union could not be attained by quite different means. One could reach the same result, for instance, by basing oneself on the profound considerations which Bernhard Welte put forward in the third volume on the Council of Chalcedon, under the title of *'homoousios hemin'*. In an ontology of the finite spirit, he showed the Hypostatic Union as the most radical (unmerited) actualization of everything that finite spirit means. From this stand-point it is easy to see that such a Hypostatic Union cannot be conceived as the merely ontic relationship between two realities conceived of as objects but, as the absolute perfection of the finite spirit as such, necessarily implies a (properly understood) 'Christology of consciousness'. In other words only in this unique, subjective unity of the human consciousness of Jesus with the Word, in the most absolute nearness, uniqueness and definitiveness, does the Hypostatic Union take place in its full reality. If one understands the relation between Hypostatic Union and *visio immediata* in this way, the latter does not need always to be expressly attested in tradition or Scripture, and the Church teaching regarding this reality receives all the same a character of necessity and obligation greater than can be given with only the help of arguments from what is fitting and proper.

If the doctrine is so deduced, we gain also a certain insight into *how* this immediacy of Jesus' human consciousness to God may be thought of. When we hear of Jesus' immediate vision of God, we involuntarily imagine this vision as an objective presentation of the divine being, which is regarded as an object opposite which the viewer stands. It comes from outside into the field of his consciousness and occupies this consciousness from outside, and hence in all its dimensions and levels. This way of conceiving things is of course not reflective, but it is thereby all the more influential in our conception of this vision of God. And when once we have this picture we imagine further—just as inarticulately and just as readily— that this divine essence which presents itself and is seen from outside is a sort of book or mirror which more or less obviously must present to the consciousness of Jesus all other possible elements of knowledge that can be thought of, and show them in their individual distinctness and their possibility of being expressed as formulated sentences.

But then we are at the problem from which we started. Can such a consciousness have been that of the historical Jesus, who we know from the Gospels had the consciousness of one who questioned, doubted, learned, was astonished, was inwardly shaken; of one who was subject to a mortal abandonment by God? But the fact is that this way of representing the immediacy of Jesus' consciousness with regard to God, which imposes itself as though it could be taken for granted, is not only not imperative, but proves itself false, if we start from the single dogmatically assured starting-point, which is all we have and which we have tried to indicate above and try from that one point to envisage the fact of this divine immediacy to consciousness. The result of this approach is that this divine immediacy, being a basic condition of the spirit of Jesus, is to be considered in the light of the substantial root of this creaturely spiritualness. For it is nothing else but the simple presence, to itself, the necessary cognizance of itself, which this substantial unity with the person of the Word possesses.

But this means that this immediate vision of God, which is really there, is absolutely nothing else but the primal, unobjectified consciousness of being Son of God, which is simply there as soon as the Hypostatic Union takes place. Since this Son-of-God-consciousness is nothing but the inner ontological luminosity of this Sonship, the subjectivity of this objective Sonship, which is necessarily given with the objective reality as its inner element. But for that very reason, this consciousness of Sonship, being its inner element, and being the immediacy to the person and being of the Word, which it necessarily implies, is not to be thought of as a way of having God before the mind as an object, towards which the thoughts of the human consciousness of Jesus would be directed, as though towards 'the other', the 'object', which stands opposite. This consciousness of Sonship and of immediacy to God, the latter not in the nature of something known only from outside but an immediacy which in absolute identity is the thing itself and its inner luminosity, is therefore situated at the subjective pole of the consciousness of Jesus.

The best way to understand it, and objectively the most correct, is to compare its nature with the subjective basic condition of the human spirit in general. This basic condition of a man, his spirituality, his transcendence, his freedom, his unity of knowledge and deed, his freely exercised understanding of self, are not first presented to him consciously when he thinks them over, reflects on them, composes sentences about them which weigh the most varying interpretations of this reality. Everywhere and always, where he exists and acts as spirit, there too where his thoughts are engaged on the most ordinary day by day external reality, this act of attending not to himself but to external objects is still inspired by this knowledge of himself, inarticulate, non-reflective, perhaps never reflected on at all. It is a simple 'self-possession' which is not reflected in clear consciousness and not translated into terms of objects, but which even when looking away from itself is still present to itself, precisely in the manner of this seemingly colourless basic condition of a spiritual being and of the horizon within which all traffic with everyday objects and concepts takes place.

This inescapable, conscious, and yet to some extent still unknown auto-lucidity, in which reality and the consciousness of it are still one undifferentiated thing, need never be the object of reflexion, may be interpreted in false concepts, and may—as always happens—be only very inadequately and asymptotically grasped. It may be interpreted from the

17

most divergent possible or impossible stand-points, and translated into the most varied terminologies and conceptual
systems, as man tries to tell himself in articulate expressions
what he already always knows (knows in that inarticulate
orientation which is the unfathomable substratum of all his
knowledge, the permanent condition of the possibility of
all other knowledge, its law and norm, its ultimate determination). This basic condition which penetrates and
moulds everything is there, and is present to consciousness,
even in men who declare that they have never had the
smallest inkling of it.

In the case of Jesus, an element of this most intimate,
primal and basic condition which is the vehicle of all
other knowledge and action is that immediacy to God
which is an inner element, subjective in nature, of the
hypostatic assumption of this human spirit, that of Jesus,
by the Word. And this conscious immediacy to God shares
the proprieties of the basic spiritual condition of the man
to whom it belongs, because ontically it is an element of
that substantial source whose presence to itself is this basic
condition in question. This immediacy to God, which is of
a conscious nature, is therefore not to be regarded as the
vision of an object. Thus the ontic and ontological thor-
oughness and completeness of this immediacy is in no way
affected. This immediacy is precisely that which we mean
when speaking of the *visio immediata*, except that any
idea of an object presented to it must be avoided, such as
we are accustomed to think of in our usual model for
representing a vision.

But on the other hand, we can in our case speak tran-
quilly and correctly of a vision, if we eliminate precisely
this objectivated 'thing in front of our thought' from the
notion. Immediacy to God is of the essence of a spiritual

person. It is an inarticulate orientation, an automatically present horizon which determines everything else, within which the whole spiritual life of this spirit takes place. It is the foundation, which can never be adequately grasped in reflexion, which bears all other spiritual actions. And being foundation, it is itself 'there' always more, and always more unlike an object, than all else, as the silent natural supposition which directs and explains everything, but cannot itself be explained, since the foundation or cause is always the clearly unclarifiable.

If we wished to have more clarity and intelligence with regard to this matter, we should have to establish and develop further the doctrine of the spiritual, inarticulate, unobjectivated and non-conceptual basic condition of a spirit. Then we could say and be better understood: the immediate presence of the Word, through itself, to the human soul of Jesus is also to be thought of in this way. But since this more general task cannot be carried any further here, we must here be content with this modest reference to a not unthinkable understanding of the absolute immediacy of the conscious communication of the Word to the human spirit of the Lord. (Hence we must deny ourselves any express treatment of the controversy between Galtier and Parente and the literature concerning it. It would involve the famous correction in the encyclical *Sempiternus Rex* between its publication in the *Osservatore Romano* and its official publication in the *Acta Apostolicae Sedis* (43, 1951). The controversy is concerned with the 'I' of Christ's consciousness, with how it is one and two-fold, and Galtier's theory of how the man Jesus knows of the Hypostatic Union. Briefly, we can say only this: According to Galtier, Jesus knows of the Hypostatic Union because he has the *Visio*; according to us, he has the *Visio* because he has the Hypostatic Union and as its inner element, the basic condition of immediacy to God.)

However, some consequences of this theory which has been put forward at least by indications may be briefly pointed out here. They will lead us back to the set of problems from which we started. If we take together what we have just stated about the nature of the conscious immediacy-to-God in Jesus, and what we said in the first introductory remark, we may proceed to say: the basic condition of immediacy to God is not merely compatible with an authentic human spiritual history and development in the man Jesus, it goes further and demands it. It is so constituted that it seeks for articulation and objectivation in spiritual concepts, not being such of itself, and leaving full room for it in the consciousness of Christ which is concerned with *a posteriori* objects.

Just as a man, in spite of his ever-present basic condition of being a spirit, in spite of the orientation given with the very foundation of his being (which has not the least thing to do with a 'feeling', though this has to be said as a precaution), has still to come to himself, has still to learn in the course of long experience to tell himself what he is and how he has already always perceived himself in the consciousness of his basic condition; just as what was always aware of itself inarticulately and unobjectivatedly, though not always consciously perceived, comes to self-awareness reflectively in terms of known objects: so it is also with Jesus' consciousness of Sonship, with his basic immediacy to God. It has been, in its spiritual history, *en route* to itself, that is, to its reflective objectivation, because the Son, by taking up a human nature, has also accepted a spiritual human history. And such a human history is not only, and not first and last, the process of being engaged with this or that outward reality. It is the asymptotic appropriation of what and who man himself is, which man already possessed himself in the depths of his being.

It is therefore quite reasonable, and not the cheap artifact of paradoxical dialectics that one should ascribe to Jesus from the beginning a basic condition of immediacy with regard to God, absolute in nature, and at the same time, a development of this primal self-consciousness by which the created spirit is absolutely orientated towards the Word. For this development is not related to the constitution of the basic condition of immediacy to God, but to the articulation and objectivation of this basic condition, which is done by reference to objects and human concepts. And this basic condition is not a knowledge expressed in multiplication of judgments; it is not a vision which has an object over against it.

These two concepts are therefore not only not mutually exclusive, they call for each other by their very nature. The basic condition or constitution wills—that is the essence of the personal history of a spirit, its total content— to communicate itself to itself. Express knowledge of its own composition, in a spiritual being, can only come to understanding of itself as the exposition and articulation of a basic condition, which is always the vehicle of such explanations and can never be totally comprehended by them, and which is, in a most hidden and intimate way, the lucidity of a spiritual reality with regard to itself. So we may speak without any embarrassment of a spiritual, indeed religious development of Jesus. It does not deny this absolute, conscious immediacy to the Word, but is borne by it, propounds it, objectivates it.

Such a progressive self-interpretation of its own basic condition by a spirit always takes place, of course, in the process of confronting the whole breadth of its outward history, as it finds itself in a milieu and exists in the midst of its surroundings. This is the material through which that which was always present to itself comes to itself. It is therefore quite legitimate to try to observe in what given world of concepts, in what eventual development—to be noted simply *a posteriori* by means of history—this gradual articulate self-possession of the God-man's basic condition, of Jesus' Sonship and immediacy to God, took place from the start. It is legitimate to trace the concepts used by Jesus, which were provided for him by his religious milieu, in order to say slowly what he already of himself knew in the depths of his being. Such a history of his self-expression does not need, at least on principle, to be interpreted only as the history of his pedagogical adaptation to his surroundings, but may calmly be read also as the history of his self-interpretation for himself.

For this does not mean that Jesus 'comes upon something' of which he knew absolutely nothing beforehand, but that he grasps ever better what he already always is and basically already knows. Whether one can say anything about this history in its details, and what exactly was its process, is not for dogmatic theology to say. In this question it is, to a certain extent, working *a priori*. It is the task of the *a posteriori* research into the life of Jesus. If it proceeds rightly, it will find nothing, at least in the material which it discovers *a posteriori*, which tells against such a primal basic condition of an absolute immediacy to God. It will perhaps even come to recognize historically that the unity of this history of the self-consciousness of Jesus, its inner continuity, clarity and imperturbability can only be sufficiently explained by this basic condition, though historically speaking, the individual items of the conceptual material, of the general background of this self-consciousness, can or could be derived to their fullest extent from the religious milieu of Jesus.

We may add to what has been said a remark about the 'infused knowledge' of Christ. Gutwenger has tried to show that there is no compelling theological reason for accepting sucn knowledge alongside the immediate vision of God and acquired knowledge. Hence one may reject the qualification of such knowledge as *sententia certa,* the note given it for instance by Ott. As far as I can see, theological reviews of Gutwenger's work have not contested his opinion in this regard. If one starts from the immediacy to God, subjective in nature, as the basic condition of Jesus' self-consciousness, and understands this consciousness as striving by its very nature to translate itself in the course of development into objectivated knowledge, we may see in this fact the objective content of what the doctrine of an (at least habitual) infused knowledge means with regard to Jesus. Thus the whole question can be quietly left as it is. For we are not bound to think of the infusion of this knowledge as though an enormous number of individual *species infusae* were poured in, but as an *a priori* cause of a knowledge which unfolds itself in meeting the reality of experience.

It may be objected against the theory outlined above that it asserts indeed a radical immediacy to God of Jesus' self-consciousness, but that it teaches—at least for the dimension of the conceptual reflexion and objectivation of this primary basic condition—a history and a development in the proper sense. And this necessarily implies stages in which certain objectivations and formulations and matters communicable of this basic condition were not yet there. Therefore, in this sense and in this dimension, there was ignorance.

We reply that such an initial ignorance is to be conceded, but we deny radically that such ignorance may not be accepted by reason of any official doctrinal declarations of the Church, or any binding theological tradition. And we must affirm that this sort of participation in history (we mean an advance from beginnings in which not everything was there in advance which should rightly only come after as an historical advance) is necessarily to be ascribed to Jesus. Otherwise the doctrine of the true, genuine humanity of the Son, which is con-substantial to our humanity would be debased to the mythology of a God disguised under the appearance of man. The doctrinal declarations of the Church tell us to maintain the immediate vision of the Word by the human soul of Jesus. They give us however no theological indications as to the exact concept of this vision of God which we are to hold. One is fully justified in saying that in this inarticulate comprehensive basic condition of Sonship and immediacy to the Word, everything is known with it, in inarticulate fashion, which pertains to the mission and the redemptive task of the Lord.

This we think does justice to the declaration in Denzinger 2184. It cannot be maintained that this text commands us to think that Jesus knew everything in the same *way* as God knew by his *scientia visionis*. Anything of the sort is completely unthinkable and is already excluded by the impossibility of a *comprehensio* of God by the human soul of Christ (*S. Th.*, III, q. 10, a. 1), since the *comprehensio* and *non-comprehensio* of God are also important for the nature and depth of the knowledge of the other possible objects. But if the difference in the modes of knowledge is once made clear, it is also clear that D 2184 is to be interpreted with circumspection and reserve.

Thereby, we also do justice to the marginal *obiter dicta* of the *magisterium* of the Church (for instance, D 2289— remembering always that the presence of a beloved person in the consciousness can be conceived of in the most varied fashions), which point in this direction. One is not thereby bound to attribute to Jesus a permanent, reflective knowledge minted in sentences, in the nature of an encyclo-paedia, or an enormous universal history actually in his mind. Here we must really see what was said in our second introductory remark: not every item of knowledge of every type is in every instant of the history of existence better than not knowing. Freedom in the space left open for decision is indeed better than the filling up of this space for freedom by a knowledge which would suffocate this freedom.

These considerations cannot be refuted by saying that they must also be valid for the basic condition of im-mediacy to God which has been put forward, and so they must be false, since they cannot be maintained there. But the basic condition is precisely such a knowledge as throws open, and does not block, this space of freedom. This transcendence towards God's infinitude—no matter how it is to be thought of more in particular, whether in our case or in the case of Christ—is, precisely in its illimitation, the condition of possibility of freedom. The transcendental anticipation of all possible objects of free action is the cause of freedom, while the objectivated, individual per-ception of all these objects in their individuation to the last degree would be the end of freedom.

This leads us finally to remark that the point of view

here adduced can throw light on the eschatological consciousness of Jesus and help to explain it more precisely. It is not the anticipation of the *Eschata*, the last things, before their time, but an outline of them drawn from the knowledge in the basic condition of his Sonship and immediacy to God. He knows these *Eschata*, and he knows them in so far as because in as much as, and in the way he knows himself as Son and his immediacy to God. In this immediacy he knows them absolutely, but as regards the objectivated communication of his immediacy, he knows them in the manner and in the measure in which this communication, which is conditioned historically and *a posteriori*, can be the vehicle of such matters.

We close this whole consideration with the formulation of a sort of thesis. It is not permissible, for the dogmatic theologian or for the exegete, to cast doubt upon the immediate vision of God by the human soul of Jesus during his earthly life. This doctrine of the *magisterium* of the Church is binding, though not a defined doctrine. Yet first of all, this does not mean that the exegete working in terms of fundamental theology (apologetics) must or can positively reckon with this theological doctrine. But further, one may think that there is a correct interpretation of his immediate vision of God which does not look on it as an extrinsic addition to the Hypostatic Union, but as understandable in itself, being an intrinsic and inevitable element of the Union. This view is held because one feels bound to understand the Hypostatic Union not merely ontically but ontologically. One can understand this vision of God as a primal and unobjectivated, inarticulated and radical basic condition of the created spirituality of Jesus. This being so, a true human experience, a historical conditioning accepted along with human nature, an authentic spiritual and religious development (which is the objectivating articulation of a primal, permanent immediacy to God, through contact with the spiritual and religious milieu and the experience of its own existence) is in every way compatible with the direct vision of God.

INDEX

Abiathar, priest 40
Abraham 150, 174f., 184–87
Acts of the Apostles 49, 68, 70, 80, 100ff., 205ff., 225f., 228, 231f.
Adam, New Adam, 52, 72, 158f.
agape 18
Amos, prophet 121
Ambrose, St 25
Angels 132, 162, 187
Apocalypse (Revelation of St John) 67, 72, 80, 103, 136, 169
Apocalypse of Baruch 163
Apocryphal gospels 223
Apologetics, *see* Fundamental Theology
Apostles 28, 47, 56, 85, 150f., 168, 220
  guarantees of historical Christ 235
  Johannine concept of 227
  Lucan concept of 226
  necessary intermediaries 235
  New Testament concept of 225
  witnesses 227f.
Apostolic preaching 205–10, 221, 225, 228, 234
Apostolic succession 77, 233f.
Augustine St 11, 12, 23, 25, 52, 157
Authority, teaching, of Church, *see* Magisterium

Baptism
  in name of Jesus 71
  Jesus' 210f.
  sins after, 70
Baptist, St John 206, 221
Bea, Cardinal 82, 108
Benedict XV, Pope 47
Biblica 126
Biblical Commission 38, 39, 84, 168
Bonaventure St 25, 113
Buddha 22
Bultmann R., 95f., 98f., 169, 209, 211f., 216f., 230

Caesar 55
Cazelles H. 194
Censure, ecclesiastical 62–64
Cerfaux L. 122
Chalcedon, Council of, 42, 51f., 124 157f., 243

Christology 41f., 48, 243
  Easter revelation of, 220
  functional 51
  Greek philosophical categories 76, 157
  implicit in words of Jesus 209, 220, 233
  kenosis problems 164ff.
  New Testament theology wider than, 107
  of Ascent 49
  of consciousness 255
  of the Resurrection 51
  ontological 51
  Old Testament 149
Chrysostom, St John 157
Church 75, 111, 125, 132, 135–37, 142, 144f., 148f., 151f., 154, 156, 225, 238
  Body of Christ 154ff.
  community of Christian faith 12, 23
  help in hearing word of Scripture 16–29, 124
  knows faith without Scripture 26
  propounds revelation 76
  organisation in New Testament 26, 77, 89
  see Magisterium, Rome, Una Sancta
Chronicles, book of, 178
Cicero 11, 28
Circumcision 185f.
Colossians, Epistle to, 156
Corinthians, Epistle to, first, 22, 23, 27, 72, 91, 100, 155, 162, 163, 170, 217, 218, 219, 225, 228f
Corinthians, Epistle to, second, 13, 14, 141, 219, 228f.
Community Theology
  includes history of redaction, 80
  limits of productivity, 202
  modifying tradition 47f., 81
  origins of, 99f
Congar Y. 143
Conzelmann H. 102
Cornelius, centurion 206
Covenant
  New 69, 189ff
  Old, biblical theme, 174, 183–192

269